A MULE, A COW & 5 JUGS OF SHINE

K.E. Wimberley

ISBN-13:9781092297592

DEDICATION

This book is for my children and grandchildren. No matter the path that you are forced to take or have taken, you can always change it and create one of your own.

ACKNOWLEDGMENTS

Thank you, Daddy, for your encouragement when I first started this book. Your proofreading and endless knowledge of the written word kept me writing. Thank you, Deana, for the long hours of reading, editing, and dedication to see this book to the end.

PROLOGUE

In the most northeastern corner of Tennessee, there is a place that time has never touched—thick with trees that have only seen those who started here, those that first settled here — air as fresh as when God first breathed life into the earth and rivers that run cleaner than any other. These mountains are where some of the first immigrants to our great country started their new life. They built houses, and began to make the best of their new homes. Bringing with them their music and a mix of cultures, they made peace with the natives of this country. Men and women came together and formed a community to raise their children. After homes had been built and wives began to give birth, the harshness of the land began to show itself. No matter how hard it became, they adapted. They successfully grew food, hunted and made tools from nature, adjusting to their new surroundings and climate. Time passed and with each generation, they faced new challenges.

In 1914, men went off to war, and afterwards returned home with the experiences of foreign places; they returned to a life that remained relatively simple and straightforward. Now being exposed to what the more advanced and prosperous parts of the world had to offer, some desired more. More money, more excitement, and more activity. During war times, many wives were left to survive the harsh life of the mountain by themselves. When husbands returned, some women walked right out of the mountains, to a better life, leaving behind their spouses and children.

Minnie Leigh's father was one man that was left to raise his children on his own. His only daughter, Minnie was the only girl out of nine children. Brothers had gone and not returned, choosing to live in modern cities or other areas of the mountain. Minnie was now left alone with her father—a man of the mountains, a man that knew nothing of the needs of a girl, or what it took to prepare her for a life outside his care. As Minnie turned thirteen, Jeremiah knew that he could no longer take care of her. And to be completely honest, he did not want to. He was bitter; bitter to the fact that he had raised nine children by himself.

The first eight had all had been young men and their needs seemed to be simple, but he had no idea what to do with a young girl.

CONTENTS

CHAPTER 1

"I am not one to sit around and recollect on memories, good or bad. But as I sit here under this great oak that has been shade for so many generations, what I see before me puts me in awe. Not just everyday awe, but swept off your feet, tears in the eye awe. I am 96-year-old, and I am looking at the answer to a prayer, prayed so long ago, and just this moment do I realize it. I have not thought of that one prayer in a long time. Why has it taken me so long to see it unfold before me, piece by piece? I guess life is like that, handed us one part at a time, something to be savored, enjoyed, and endured. A little learning here, a little learning there; a relationship, a child, and maybe another. What finite eyes we have. You can never see the blessing of life as it is coming together, you can only see it when it is finished. Oh, my! What joy to have all the inner turmoil I once felt melt away in one glance of God's unfolding plan."

As I looked across the vast lawn, there sat at various places, in different groups, my children and grandchildren playing cards, or laughing at Steven telling some joke or crazy story. Another group was being entertained by music as Tristen taught some of the younger ones to play the early mountain gospel songs we used to sing. MaryJane and Georgia Rose, my two southern bells, were sitting on a quilt all proper, playing with my newborn grandson. How content she was, how fulfilled.

As my eyes once again took in the sight of my family's home place—the house, the outbuildings, and the path that led from the thick of the woods—the scene caused a flood of memories to come rolling in like scenes from a projector.

The path that I walk from gathering Ginseng, one cold fall morning, I feel won't ever turn out right once I am forced to walk it. It is a path I walk just to arrive full circle back where I started. I don't know if my father would approve or not, but here I am, his only daughter, left with more than he first traded me for. God is just showing me once again that He is in control. No matter what our perception of our circumstances is or what life deals us at the start, He can always turn sour to sweet, bitter to something to be savored, and iron to gold.

I was brought out of my daydream by my granddaughter Nicole.

"You look very content Grams; you're glowing. I guess with all you have, and when life is so easy and simple, why not? You have someone who's devoted and loves you very much."

"You'ins should never assume anything child. Not even when it comes to family," I said.

"Why Grams, you and Papaw have always been happy. Even when I was a young child, you two were always laughing and carrying on like teenagers sweet on each other. I guess that comes easy when you have known someone all your life. There seems to be a bond that forms deeper roots."

"*Ha!* See? Told you'ins never to assume things, child. You still have a lot to learn, but there's still time, it's never too late. See, your Papaw and I didn't meet each other until I was thirty-one."

"*What?*" Nicole said with surprise. "I have always thought —" she paused to count on her fingers, "I have never stopped and thought about it but if this is your sixty-fifth wedding anniversary and you are...*wow*, guess that adds up." I laughed to herself as my grand-daughter rambled on about Papaw being just eighty-six. Nicole was laughing, realizing for the first time, that he was much younger than his bride.

CHAPTER 2

Following a short story that won a scholarship for a local young lady, I have become somewhat of a novelty. I never thought about my story, never thought about it at all. To me, it was just my life, and I did the best I knew how to do.

I used to enjoy stopping on the street while in town, to speak to an old friend or even making a new one, by striking up a conversation. Now, I am scared of what they may ask, so I turn away. I don't want to dig up my past anymore. The good book says to not worry about yesterday or tomorrow; they have enough worries of their own. How right it is; yesterdays are hard to think about and tomorrow, well, tomorrow ain't here yet—don't know what will happen.

Most people don't know much about East Tennessee, and its place in American History. Usually, they only conjure up the pictures of moonshine, and barefoot, dirty, illiterate hillbillies. What's most overlooked is those same families that were barefoot, and lived by themselves outside of the "modern world," had a good reason as far as they were concerned.

Before established towns and governments were formed, these families were the first settlers in these mountains. White, black, Irish, and Scott, they lived together and thrived peacefully. That is, until the outside world started creeping in with land grabs and the search for gold. From then, up to their present-day descendants, they've been threatened by Indians, or angered by broken treaties and greedy men seeking to make themselves wealthy at any cost.

Cornwallis, leader of the defeated British army, and those

who moved to this area—with power and money enough to drive those families higher up into the mountains and away from their farms—were all very surprised at their intellect and resilience. They thought the mountain people would give in to fear or die of poverty. Never did they believe these people would become some the strongest or longest surviving descendants of our America's first families.

Elizabethton, Mountain City, and Del Rio are the name of some of our towns, and unless you're a history buff, you may not know that it's here that the first independent settlement and government was formed, outside the thirteen colonies. The Watauga Association was created in 1772 and was the first to draw up a declaration of independence known as the Watauga Documents. Signers and members of this declaration were members of this settlement, and declared their freedom and independence before the Declaration of Independence of 1776.

There are people of distinction from every walk of life, from East Tennessee, who changed history. You have Davy Crockett: pioneer, politician, the hero of the Alamo. Tennessee Ernie Ford: singer and actor born and raised in Bristol Tennessee. Grace More: one of the world's greatest opera singers from Slabtown Tennessee, which is now part of Del Rio. She was also a very accomplished actress. James Agee: born in Knoxville Tennessee, and a Pulitzer Prize winner. No one can even mention Tennessee without thinking of Dolly Parton: singer, actress, producer, national treasure. It's a list that's way too long for me to quote. But the point is that the perception others may have of the East Tennessee Hillbilly is a perception that should never make one ashamed.

East Tennessee also has a dark side, or so they say, with its moonshine stories and the history Johnson City played. It was known as Little Chicago for a time, due to a significant amount of illegal liquor Al Capone moved through the area. One of the biggest suppliers for Al Capone's men during prohibition were the moonshiners of East Tennessee. It was common knowledge that Capone stored most, if not all, of the illegal liquor in his

Johnson City operation. However, I might not have all that entirely accurate, but I do know my Paw had some mighty highfalutin friends that would meet him at the bottom of the mountain. They were in their fancy suits and ties, and I remember they wore those funny looking shoe covers, Spats I believe they were called.

Once in a while, I would make the trip down the mountain and, once or twice, all the way to Johnson City. You would think my Paw would have had enough money to buy the U.S. itself. But somehow, he was still always in want for more of this, or more of that. It was on one such trip that my father made the acquaintance of Tolbert, and from there, an idea began to form on how he could change his plight as he saw it.

CHAPTER 3

"God, I've been told that you made all things. If'in that's true, you sure-fire knows what you'ins doin. I sure like how that sun up there comes peekin' thru the leaves while the dew is still a layin', and the sun shines through the mist in the early morn. Why, it's the best time of the day. That's why I enjoy doing my diggin' in the mornin' time so's I can see that big old sun wakin' up. Some days it comes risin' over the mountain with evera color there ever has been. Lookin' down across the valley, it looks like a field of diamonds, and jewels. And that waterfall looks like I could pinch it up in my hand and take it with me. Yes, God, you must have made all things causin' if you didn't, I sure fire can't figure out how all this bounty got here.

"Well, I guess I best get goin'. Paw goin' to wonder where I got off too for so long. Paw don't take to day-dreamers. Well, if you'ins is there, thank you, see you in the morn."

In clothes too big for her—one of Paw's shirts and pants that were synched up with braided hide from deer, bear, or one of the many animals trapped here on the mountain—and unkept strawberry blond hair covered by an old hat found on some trail, Minnie Leigh cleared the thick of the woods onto a path that led to the front of the cabin her and her Paw shared.

As Minnie, humming from contentment, cleared the front corner of the cabin, there stood Paw with some stranger. She stopped abruptly, as she never interfered with man folk's talk. Then, backing slowly up, she froze when her Paw yelled out: "Minnie Leigh, come here gal!"

"Yes, Paw?"

"Minnie Leigh, go pack your things. This here are your'ins a husband," he says as he points to the stranger. "You'in is goin' with him."

Still frozen in her tracks, Minnie asked, "What you'in talkin' 'bout, Paw? I don't have no husband!"

"You'in does now! Go fetch your'un things gal, do as I say."

"Paw, this here man is an ol' man! I ain't wanted to marry no ol' man. Sides, where is the preacher that mar'id us?"

"You'in already marr'ed to him gal, 'cause I say so. I don't need no preacher to tells me who I gives you'ins too. *Now go!* Get your'ins things as I said."

Dazed, Minnie walked into the house, more like someone that just had a spell put on them than one moving under their own power.

I must be a dreamin', is all's I know this here ain't real, it can't be. My paw wouldn't just toss me off like any old animal, like old bath water, she walked back out of the house with a small pack containing all she owned, her face blank.

"This here's Tolbert. He's now your'ins husband. Go with him, make you'ins self a good life. I be seein' you'ins." Then Paw walked off around the cabin, bowed up like he did when the federal man came snoopin' around.

As Minnie Leigh stared after her paw in shock, the stranger gave her a shove to get her stepping.

"Don't be a shovin' me!" Minnie snapped, but kept moving.

"Let's get somethin' straight, gal, before we start out. You'ins going to do what's you'ins are told. We ain't havi'n no fussin' back and far'ths. Get movin', we need to be gettin' so we get home for dark."

They walked along the path thru the woods, a clearing, then back through more woods and another clearing. After an hour or so, Minnie suddenly stopped, and turned quickly. She started to head back from the direction she came, back toward home, without a second thought.

Tolbert grabbed her by the arm. "Now just where do

you'ins think you'ins a goin'?"

"I'm a headin' back home to see just what Paw is really up to."

Tolbert turned Minnie abruptly in her tracks, his fingers digging into her skin. "*Up to?!* What you'ins mean *up to?*"

"Well, I don't 'member marry *no one*! Especially not no old man," she grumbled loudly.

"You was given in trade. I needed a wife, and your Paw been in want of my farmland up here. Bein' I never come this far up, seems like good as time as any to get myself a wife, and your'ins Paw to get some land. So, I came on up here and got rid of land I don't use, and looks like I gots me a purtty wife for my trouble. Now turn and get movin', done told you'ins I want to get home before dark!" he rambled on.

"Trade? *Trade?* I ain't no animal, or piece of hide to be traded like next year's beef or salt meat!" Minnie Leigh just stood there, in disbelief of all that had transpired over the last couple of hours. How could her Paw who loved her just trade her like she ain't nothin'? *Less he don't love me at all. Can't be no other reason.*

Suddenly, she was jerked with violent force, as Tolbert grabbed her by her hair and spun to slap her angrily, growing impatient of her idleness.

"You'ins is a female. What you say don't 'mount to a hill of beans less'in' a man says it does! You is my *wife*, and that's that, so's get movin'!"

Tolbert pushed Minnie ahead of him. She stumbled, but was determined not to show weakness. Minnie managed to keep herself upright, and labored forward with a heart full of anger and hurt, tears of disbelief streaming down her face in silence.

Up and over the hills, through a steep hollow back up another, they walked as the sun began to dip below the tree line. They climbed a steep winding path that opened into a clearing where a less-than-inhabitable looking cabin sat. Even worse, there was a corral that was attached to the house.

"Why're the animals right next to the house?" Minnie suddenly asked, breaking the silence that had formed between them. "Bet it smells like a bed of lilies in that th'ar cabin," She mouthed with full-on sarcasm.

"No sass. You don't like where I have animals kept, I'll show you how to saw lumber, and you can build yourself a new barn and corral and put it any place you see fit," the man grumbled.

They made their way to the cabin, and climbed a set of steps that were in ill repair. Minnie feared they might not even hold her small frame, and stepped carefully.

Once inside, Tolbert went straight to the wood stove, and stoked up the fire with wood. "The stove will be hot shortly. Get some food cooking. I'll be back in as soon as I throw some grain to the livestock. Scratch around and use what's here. I'm powerful hungry," he said offhandedly, as if nothing had happened.

Minnie Leigh, still stunned by the day's events, didn't know where to begin. Looking on the shelves and in various cans, she was able to produce a small batch of biscuits and gravy from lard and flour. When Tolbert returned, the biscuits and gravy along with deer jerky had been laid out on the table.

They ate in silence. However, Minnie noticed Tolbert staring at her with a twisted grin on his face.

"You'ins sleep over th'ar on that bed for now. It'll do 'til I can build one big enough for both of us," he sneered.

"*Us?!* I want never be sleepin' with you!" her eyes widened, her body flinching away.

"Oh yes you will, gal. You'ins is my wife now," he reminded her. But then his smile twisted again. "Let's just get this straightened out now." H bolted toward Minnie, grabbing her arm before twisting it behind her. Tolbert wasted no time pushing her to the bed.

Tolbert held Minnie down as he brutally raped her. Her screams and attempts to fight him off didn't faze him. It was if he didn't hear her, and it was over as soon as it began. He stood up, not caring as Minnie laid confused, bruised, and crying.

Tolbert simply turned and left the cabin, slamming the door behind him.

CHAPTER 4

Waking after a night of fitful sleep on a corn cob mattress, one feels every lump and bump straight to the bone. Minnie had heard tell of people sleeping on these things, but never made sense to her why someone would use corn cobs. Now she was convinced she was right. *Makes no sense, no sense at all.* As she looked around, her new home looked even more dismal in the daylight than it had in the candlelight. *There must be twelve inches of dirt on the floor*, she thought, and thought about nothing else.

"Guess I better find where to fetch some water. I ain't got nowhere else to live, might as well make this one as clean as I can."

Stepping out of the rear door, Minnie found herself on a wide porch. At one end, there was a door with a lock, and the windows boarded up from the inside. "Now what you suppose a person like Tolbert got that needs lockin' up? I sure aim to find out, but I best being straightened things up first."

Glancing around and seeing no movement, Minnie got the feeling that Tolbert was nowhere to be found. "Figures he would disappear and leave me to all this here mess. Well, I got to pass the time somehow, and I ain't livin' like no bunch of hogs." She pushed up her sleeves, and went straight to work.

Minnie Leigh soon found a stream, not far from the cabin, where she would haul water. She had seen a feed bucket that would suffice for now, though she would have to have Tolbert fetch a few things for her if he expected her to take care of his home properly. She first filled the water trough for the horses and cows, then she threw some hay and feed to them. After that, she began hauling water to the house.

A couple of hours later, standing in the doorway inspecting her work, she felt a sense of pride in having a clean home. The way it came about still made her sick to her stomach, but she pushed the thoughts away, and figured she would make the best she could with where she found herself. Her paw sure didn't want her, and this here man did, even though he was much older than her. What other choices did she have?

But turning to survey the outside and the work there was to do, she suddenly became overwhelmed with the prospect of doing it all on her own.

"Wonder where that man is? I don't want to get in the middle of his farm. Don't mind helpin', but I done learned a long time ago not to get in the midst of a man's business. All that scrubbing and warshin' on the inside done plum wore me out. Guess it won't hurt if I sit a spell."

Taking a seat on a stool next to the door, Minnie leaned her head back to enjoy the cool of the shade that had begun to fall on the porch. As she was relaxing a bit, her eyes closed in daydream. But she was brought back when she heard footsteps approaching.

"Howdy ma'am. Well my, my. I heard old Tolbert done got him a wife, but ain't heard he got a child too."

"I'm not a child, I *am* his wife!"

"You a young'un. You can't be no one's wife, 'special' not Tolbert's. Why, he's forty or more!" the man raised an eyebrow.

"I may not be old enough to be his wife, but ain't no young'un. I am thirteen and full grown," Minnie asserted.

"Child, you're a young'un, and your'in needs to be whupped for sassin' a grown man. You'ins a female too. You'ins should know better than usin' snappy words when you speak to me," the man's eyes narrowed in annoyance.

Now, scared by the abruptness of the stranger, Minnie tried to move him along, "Tolbert ain't here. What's your'ins name? I'll let him know you'ins stopped by."

His eyes stayed narrowed. "No need child, just wanted to say howdy. I sure I will be seein' him sooner or later."

As the stranger disappeared into the woods, Minnie jumped to her feet, and went about looking for a knife or gun she might use as protection.

"I better not be nappin' again, coulda got myself hurt." Finding an ax, Minnie started a new job, and began to cut saplings at the edge of the woods to make new railings for the garden and corral fences. She kept the house in sight as not to wander too far off.

After a while, she raised her hand over her eyes to shield them from the sun. Minnie guessed the time to be about mid-morning. "Seems this here day is movin' mighty slow, but I got the house done and the garden fence. This corral should be finished a'for' dinner' time. I best leave Tolbert somethin' to do. He might get mad me for fixin' all these things around here. Seems he likes 'em in a broke down mess though."

Then Minnie smiled to herself, and laughed out loud.

"What you'ins laughin' at, gal? You done lost you'ins senses?"

Startled, Minnie spun around to find Tolbert propped against the fence post with a jug thrown over his shoulder. "Well, don't just stand th'ar, gal. All this work ain't go'in to get finished with you'in standin' idle."

"Me? Don't you'ins mean *us?* Since we are supposed to be husband and wife, this herein is our place, and we should work together to make it a home," she reminded him.

"Gal, you do what I tell you to do. Don't be getting' no fancy ideas in that head of your'ins, just cause your'in is my wife. This here place is *mine.* All you have to do is keep it nice, and have me a slew of boys I can leave it to. That's a woman's job on this earth. Nothin' else," he spat, watching her slowly.

Minnie was uneducated, but she knew enough not to challenge this man with nowhere for her to go. She remembered the burning and ache of her face and jaw when he slapped her on their journey here. Not to mention the brutal way he had handled her last night.

With long, slow strides, Tolbert made his way to the porch where he could catch some shade. He propped himself against a porch rail to keep an eye on Minnie as she worked. "I want that garden area cleared next, gal, so you can put some seed in the ground tomorrow. 'Bout waited too long to get them in the ground now. Be sure and pile the stones you plow out up yonder on that wall. It keeps the hillside from warshin' into the house."

"*Sons?*" Minnie said under her breath, still stuck on the thought. "I won't be havin' you'in no sons or daughters."

"What's that you said, gal?" Tolbert raised his voice.

"Nothin', I ain't said nothin'," she shook her head.

"Well, you'ins better not be. I won't have no grumblin' when I done been so kind as to bring you'ins up here and give you'ins a home."

Minnie kept silent despite his lie and continued working, fitting the rails to the corral fence. With Tolbert's help, the job could have gone smoother and quicker. But Minnie was not one to complain or give up on things so quickly. She would keep at it until it was finished and finished right.

Again, shading her eyes from the full force of the sun, she gaged the time to now be mid-afternoon. Tolbert appeared to be passed out, so Minnie took off toward the creek where she drew water that morning.

Cooling herself and replenishing what she had sweated out, she lay back in the leaves on the bank, glad to be away from him. Minnie stared up through the trees, and realized she had not greeted the morning.

"Hello day, hello God. Seems like you must've not been awake to listen to me yesterday mornin', 'cause right after I finished talkin' to you'ins, everything turned upside down. This here's a beautiful day, but why you let my Paw trade me like I was nothin'? I don't recall doin' nothin' that was all bad, but whatever it was, could you kindly forgive me? Take this here mess and straighten it out for me."

"Gal! Hey, gal!" Minnie heard Tolbert bellowing. "Where'd you run to, gal? You better not have run off, 'cause me and your'ins Paw done made a deal. You'ins remember that you'ins can't leave here unless I say you can!"

"Quit your hollerin' like an old sow. I just gettin' some water and coolin' off a minute," Minnie bellowed back while standing to brush off her britches and shake out her old hat.

As she cleared the woods and started to look up to the house, Minnie felt herself falling, and her face burned and ached as it never had before. "You'ins are going to learn to quit sassin', gal!" he shouted through the slap. "I don't care *what* you'ins Paw use to do. Round here, you don't talk back to no man. I heard how you'in treated my company that come around this mornin'. Don't you'in *ever* shame me like that again!"

"I ain't goin' to be hit on all the time!" Minnie screamed through her tears, trying to be brave.

Tolbert reached out, and took Minnie by the hair. He pulled her to the house kicking and screaming the whole way. By the time he dropped her by the steps, her scalp was bleeding, her body was scratched, and she was cut and bruised all over again.

"You'ins will be whatever I say. If I feels like you'in needs the sass beat out of you'in, that's what you'in will get! You'ins keep forgetin' you's a *gal*. Now wash you'ins face, and get back to work, gal. Get that garden ready to plant in the morn. Don't let me hear you'in make a sound, and you'ins better have me some food on that table when I return," he hollered, then disappeared again.

Several minutes later, with her head throbbing and bleeding from cuts and scratches, Minnie hitched one of the horses to the plow harness. Leading him to the garden area, she backed him up to the plow rig. Stepping into place, she fixed the strap over her head, and across her shoulder, giving the strap a tug and a command to the horse so he would begin to pull. Minnie pointed the blade into the ground, letting it slice the soil open to reveal deep rich, black earth.

Now, in the mountains of east Tennessee, if you are going to farm the mountainside, now and again you are going to hit a rock, stone, or even boulders. Now and then, Minnie had to move a rock, but as she was finishing, she hit something that would not budge.

She sighed, and returned to the barn to find a pick-ax or something to help her remove the large boulder. But as she got near the barn, she saw another stranger standing propped up on the rail of the corral fence. He was just standing there, watching her as she approached him.

"Who are you'ins? What you'ins want?" she asked warily.

"Ishmael, ma'am," he nodded. "Just come by on some business with Tolbert. Ma'am. Are you ok? You'ins have been bleedin'."

Minnie had forgotten about her appearance until now. She had been hit and thrown around so much since she arrived, the aches and pain had all run together. Still, her mind drifted to the task at hand: plowing in the hot sun. Even though she was aware of the pain, focusing on work had helped it dull.

"I'm alright. I took a tumble earlier and forgot bout cleanin' myself up. I been tryin' to finish this plowin'. I down to last three rows, and I seem to have struck something big this time. Guess them seeds Tolbert wanted in the ground tomorrow will have to wait 'til I can talk him into helpin' me get it out of there," she shrugged, trying to be friendly to not to make Tolbert mad again.

"Well ma'am, I don't mind helpin'. That's how we do up here, we help out when we come along and find someone needs us," he smiled a bit.

Minnie thought about it, but shook her head. "Thanks, but I better try and do it myself. If Tolbert comes home, he won't take kindly to me talkin' and workin' with you."

"You let me worry 'bout what Tolbert says and does if he comes walkin' up. Let me see what this here horse and I can do together. He and I might be able to pull this boulder on up and get it out of the way," Ishmael walked over to her.

After loosening the soil around the boulder with the pick and shovel, he hitched his horse up with the other horse. Together, Minnie and the man tugged, pried, and hooves clawed deep. Working with the two horses, the boulder was easily pulled from the ground. He let them drag it a couple of yards away, unhitched the horses, and gave them water for a job well done. Minnie said nothing while he made the ground even.

She took her horse by the lead, and hitched him back to the plow with a pat on the neck. "Sorry boy, I got these three rows to finish. I hate to ask you'ins after the hard work you'ins done put in, but let's get it done, and I'll give you some extra feed, water, and a good brushing."

Watching Minnie as she started plowing again, Ishmael yelled after her: "Tell Tolbert I come by to fetch my batch. I'll come on back in the next couple of days. I be seein' you'ins." He walked back towards the woods leading his horse, but as Ishmael was disappearing, she gave a wave and a thank you.

Ishmael walked on scratching his head. *Now, I wonder why Tolbert has that gal, so small and young, up here. Wonder who she is. Just where do you find someone like her?*

After feeding the horse and rubbing him down just as she promised, Minnie threw feed to the other animals, and shut up the hen house for the night. As she walked into the house, she wondered what Ishmael had meant by *his batch*. She also noticed the sun getting low in the sky, and could hear the whippoorwill singing. Minnie quickened her step, as she had not even started the fire in the stove.

"Hope th'ars some taters and onion to stir together. Maybe some cornmeal for some corn pone. Hope that man ain't too hungry, 'cause it sure takes a while to cook up a full meal," she said out loud.

Minnie quickly got the big wood stove fire burning, and the iron plate on top began heating up. She put lard in the black cast iron skillet she found hanging on the wall, and potatoes and onions were diced up and placed in the hot grease. Once she finished frying the potato and onions, she fried the cornmeal into corn pone patties just like her Paw taught her to do. Everything was covered and pushed to the back of the stove to keep it warm before Tolbert was back.

"It feels like I'm here a month already, and this here just the end of the first day. I'll be dead from work in a month."

Minnie didn't bother with cleaning herself up. She was used to it until the summer got there. The water in the creeks and river was still cold, and could kill you if you tried to bathe off every day. Why, someone would get sick bathing that much. She was also very tired.

Minnie didn't even remember shutting her eyes after she laid down on the corn-cob mattress that she'd placed on the floor near the stove. Sometime in the night though, she woke to the sound of someone stumbling around the table.

It was Tolbert snickering and talking to himself. "I will have this place clean and lookin' like some fancy lowland farm. I got that gal scared out her mind now. Yep, everything should be ready, and all washed up just in time."

Just in time for what? thought Minnie. But once again, sleep overtook her before she had a chance to fully think it out.

CHAPTER 5

Tolbert Regan was not a working man, but he'd been very ambitious. At the age of fourteen, he was already known for his quality moonshine, and outfoxing the federal men. He bought up an excellent piece of land and retired from moonshining, as far as anybody could swear to. At thirty, he had already acquired a small fortune, enough for him to live on without ever working again.

The last time Tolbert was seen doing any hard work was when he was building his cabin with a lean-to barn on one side. Said there was no need to traipse across near fifty or a hundred yards to feed some animals when you could just step out your front door, and toss them some food just a few feet away.

He was not born in this part of the mountain. His father had moved him and his two brothers and sister there after their Maw died. No one could figure out why old man Regan would up and leave the land he was born to. Nevertheless, his father packed them up and moved away from Roane Mountain, then bought the small plot of land for more than it was worth. Tolbert was twelve years old when they made that move.

Two years later, everyone knew Tolbert. If you wanted moonshine, you got it from Tolbert.

Now, no one could ever prove anything, but even though Tolbert took credit for making the shine, everyone expected his Paw was involved. The federal men hated the Regans because they could never find any evidence; no still, no jars, no jugs, not even enough grain to feed their mangy livestock, much less make a batch of shine. But when a local went to purchase a jar or jug, Tolbert would disappear into the woods, and was back in a blink of an eye just as if he'd taken it off a shelf or something. Tolbert was as sneaky and sly as they come.

It was said Tolbert traded off his birth land, near six acres. Traded it off for the wife he had up there. Most folks would say it was the only way he could get a wife. Everyone in this part of the mountain knew how he treated women.

His kinfolk said when he was a very young boy, he took the hoe handle after his Maw. She told him to finish hoeing the garden, and he just didn't feel like doin' any more hoeing. She tried to scold him for sitting when he broke the handle off. He went after his Maw, swinging wild, not caring who he might hurt. Meaner than an old momma bear he was.

As Tolbert joined his friends at the state line tavern, the questions started flying.

"Whose daughter you done stole, Tolbert? Ain't no man in his right mind goin' to give you his daughter's hand in ma-tray-mona to you!"

"That th'ar mail-order bride of you'ins; he sure is young and purty, Tolbert. How much did she cost you'ins? *Ha ha!*"

"Yea, 'cause we know she didn't choose you'ins of her own free will."

"You'ins is just jealous cause I got a female the dogs don't run from. Sides, I got a plan! You'ins just wait and see. You won't be a laughin' too long. You'ins have to work, but I'm retired. I don't have to work, 'specially now I got me someone to fix my place up for me."

"Retired? You'ins ain't never worked 'cept makin' some shine and haulin' it out of the mountain. Selling moonshine to those valley folks? That there ain't no hard work. And since when you'ins been worried what you'ins place looks like?"

Tolbert, becoming furious, threw his jug at the group of men. "I do work! I've been workin' since I was a young man. How do you think that corn and fixin's got into that still? Fools! Your'ins are nothin' but some fools!"

Tolbert left, stomping down the trail toward his home.

The further he went, the madder he got.

"Now, how they know all 'bouts my business?"

As he approached his house, he suddenly couldn't believe the work this one little gal had done. He stepped up on the porch, and peered inside. "Well I'll be. This cabin ain't never been this clean, not even when I first put it up. This plan comin' 'bout faster than I thought"

Tolbert turned and took back up the trail. Soon, he was at the house of Lilly Mae.

Now, Lilly was the gal all the menfolk were waiting on to grow up. She was a healthy and robust girl, but somehow managed to always look like she never did any hard work at all. Skin lily white, and hair soft as cotton and red as wild raspberries. Her eyes were golden brown. But Lilly Mae's Paw owned the best plot of land on the mountain, and the biggest. He was making her wait to marry 'til she was almost too old to marry, but he wouldn't let her marry just anybody.

See, most folks up here, when the daughter marries, they move off to the man's property. But Lilly's Paw wanted his daughter and husband-to-be to live at least a year nearby, if not with him and Lilly's Maw. Wanted to make sure she was taken care of. The only exception was if the man had a secure home, and was fit for Lilly to live as she had been brought up.

Now, her Paw didn't know it, but she and Tolbert had been meeting in the moonlight making plans. Tolbert had his eye on her since she was born, and the plot of land her Paw owned was worth more gold than anyone in the world had.

Whistling their secret whistle, Tolbert stood just back of Lilly's homestead. He whistled several more times before she appeared.

"What you doin' here in the daylight? You want my Paw to shoot you?"

"No, no, I had to come. I have news."

"Yea! I done heard, you know," Lily said, turning her back toward him and crossing her arms with a huff. "You have some *nerve* showin' up here. Done moved a woman in. Says she's your *wife*. What, I ain't worth waitin' for no more?"

"Yes, Lilly, you are. She's all part of the plan! See, your Paw won't let you marry me 'cause he says I'm a no-good, lazy shiner. Well, this here girl was payment on a trade. She not my wife. She down there right now cleanin' and shinin' things up, and tomorrow the garden will be planted. Then I'm going to invite your Paw over to see that I ain't lazy. Place be spit-shined, and he'll be proud to have me as his son-in-law."

"Well, how ya' gone explain her doin' all the work?"

"Only two folks seen her doin' any work. One won't talk, and the other I think I can make a trade with him he can't refuse."

Lilly turned back around and jumped at him, throwing her arms around his neck. "You're a rascal, Tolbert Regan, but long as I have my own place, I don't care how's I get it. Tired of all these mountain girls sayin' Paw spoon feedin' me even though I'm grown woman! Just wait 'til they all hear 'bout you'ins and me."

"Can't wait?" Tolbert asked sarcastically, which Lily never caught. She was just spoiled, and wanted what she wanted. It had never crossed her mind that she meant no more to Tolbert except what he could gain from her.

Back on the trail, whistling from his perceived success, Tolbert headed back to his farm to make sure things got done right and fast.

CHAPTER 6

Now what you suppose Tolbert's up to with that young girl? She's workin' and sweatin' like a slave. Maybe the rumors about him and Lilly ain't right. Maybe he done found someone else.

Couldn't be, he thought. *That young'un can't be eleven, twelve years old. Well, she too young to be his bride! Her husband shouldn't be any older than twenty, thirty at the most. She a might purty gal though. Wonder where he found her?* he thought. *Maybe she has an older sister, or younger one that could be courted 'til she old enough to marry.*

Ishmael was one of nine, number three in the line of seven sons and two daughters, sort of a loner when it came to his family. Even though he had not married, he moved out at twenty and built himself a small cabin on the far side of his family's land at the foot of a waterfall. He cleared the area and set the cabin just where you could look out the window, or sit on the porch, and see the falls and the sun setting behind the mountain. It was a place he'd gone to all his life. He dreamed of having this cabin, a pretty wife, and a slew of kids just like his Paw.

Ishmael grew up in a good home of churchgoers. No one was running moonshine. His parents raised some good crops, and fattened cattle and hog every year. His Paw even went to the valley from time to time to help out with odd jobs to be able to buy store-bought clothes and books for his children.

But since Ishmael had been out on his own, he had been late for church a lot, and even missed a service once in a while. If his Maw knew the truth why he wasn't there, he was sure she'd tan his hide even though he was a full-grown man.

Shining was just a way of life up here. He'd never seen his Paw take more than one sip and walk away. More for just being sociable than for the enjoyment of it. Matter of fact to hear it, his Paw kicked up some trouble around here in his day.

Then he saw Ishmael's Maw. His Paw started out flirting and being loud, showing off, as he did for all the other girls. But she'd just turn her head in embarrassment, and pay him no mind. So, he started asking the other girls about her, trying to find out what she liked and what kind of husband she wanted 'cause he was determined that was going to be his wife.

That's when his Paw changed his ways. He started going to church, and before you knew it, he was listening to the preacher for real. He started reading the good book, learned all he could about this God of Abraham, Isaac, and Jacob. Then one Sunday before singing got started, there he was down front on his knees, and everyone was gathering around him, laying their hands on him to pray for his soul.

Ishmael shook his head, and smiled thinking about his Paw that way. *I just don't understand how a strong man like my Paw could believe all those Bible stories and all the begetting.*

Now, when it came to a girl like that one up there at Tolbert's, that could be understood. Her sturdy stature and that fire red hair—real red, not that orange, like his brother had. No, that girl had hair as red as blood, and her eyes seemed to be made of glass—now, *that* was the kind of girl you could change for, not someone like a Maw. Maw was purty and all, but Maw, well... Maw was *Maw*.

Now, as Ishmael was sittin' there, watchin' the sunset behind the mountain and the night sky start to appear, Tolbert came walk' in out of the woods carting a couple of jugs of shine.

"Hey, Ishmael."

"Hey, Tolbert. What you doin' roamin' around this way? Oh! You'ins must have gotten my message," Ishmael smiled.

"Message? What message?" asked Tolbert as he squinted.

"I told that gal to let you know I come after my batch."

"When did you see her?" the man grumbled.

"Oh, not a few hours ago," Ishmael shrugged. "She done run up on some trouble plowin' when I walked up. So, I helped out a might."

"You did, did ya? Help out, you said? Well, that better be all you did," Tolbert grumbled louder, his eyebrows knitted.

"I swear to ya, that's all I did. We pulled a stone out the ground 'bout the size of a wagon wheel, and heavier than twenty full grown hogs. Then I filled in the dirt so's the ground wouldn't be uneven, and busted up a couple of bales of hay over it to finish fillin' the hole as was a might short on dirt."

"Well, I guess that be alright," he shrugged. "Long as you sure that's all, 'cause I got plans for that gal."

"Yea, I know you'in a plan to marry that purty thang and set up house. Can't say as I blame you though, 'cause if she had a sister, I am settin' up house too," Ishmael hooted.

"You'in would, would ya?" Tolbert said slowly.

"Well, um, yeah…um," he saw the look on the other man's face. "Awe, come on Tolbert, don't be getting all riled up. I just makin' talk."

Tolbert held out one of the jugs, and picked the other up with a smile. He slung it over his shoulder, and took a big pull of liquor. Ishmael did the same, and the night got started. Before you knew it, they were both wasted and laughing and singing. Then Tolbert stood up and walked around in front of Ishmael.

"Ishmael, I got an idea how you can get you a gal just like the one I got. No, not just like her, but *her*."

"Why? She got a sister you can get for me?" he asked, confused.

"No," Tolbert slurred. "I mean, I got a plan for you'ins, and if you'ins can help, then, you'ins can *have* her."

"Have her? What you'ins mean?" Ishmael was excited now.

"Well," Tolbert said, "she done…done such a good job 'round my farm today, it got me thinkin'. I have been wantin' to get hitched to Lilly for a long time now. Now her Paw is ready to give her hand, and this here gal comes along. Bad timin', just bad timin'," he twisted the truth.

"Hold on now," Ishmael slurred back. "Let's talk 'bout this a little more. If you'ins goin' to get rid of her, I might just be instrid in dealin'."

"Okay, here what I's been sittin' here thinkin'—"

Now as the night waned to early morning, a plan was hatched so that both men could get the bride they were wanted.

CHAPTER 7

Minnie Leigh woke with a start. The sun wasn't up yet, but something just wasn't right. Change in the air? No, maybe something inside of her telling her, preparing her.

Minnie stood up on the cold cabin floor and took a deep breath. She reached for the wood beside the stove to stoke the fire, then noticed that the frying pan was now empty.

She spun around to see Tolbert sprawled out on his bed with clothes, boots, and all still on like the day before. *Passed out from too much drink*, thought Minnie. *Never knowed someone could drink shine all the time. No wonder this place be run down.*

Minnie picked up her shoes, and stepped out the door into the early morning air. Taking a deep breath, she felt refreshed on the inside, but her aching body brought back the memories of the day before, all the hard work, and not to mention being drug from the creek by her hair. The scalp was still sore.

Down the steps, and slipping on her shoes, she walked to the corral just a few feet away. But as she reached the gate, she thought, *On second thought, I think I'm going down to that creek and lay back in the leaves and greet the morning, just like I use to at home.* She quickly grabbed the bucket to bring back water for livestock and coffee.

As Minnie lay there in the cool of the morning, she prayed. "Now God, I already told ya I wasn't sure you were real, and now here I am, miserable and hurtin', and I have nowhere to go. My Paw done traded me off. How am I supposed to believe you'ins is real if you'ins keep letting all this happen to me? All I want is to have a home here in the mountain with a good man, a church goin' man to love me, and happy, healthy children and grand-kids that love me. Laughin' and smilin', enjoying each other the way we s'pose' to. You s'pose' that too much to ask for?"

Then light began to break through the lower edges of the trees. Minnie jumped, knowing she had a lot to do, and since she didn't want to get hit again, she better be getting back to the house.

Stopping back by the corral, she threw some hay and feed to the livestock, and poured most of the water in the tough she had brought back from the creek. Next, stepping inside as quiet as she could, she poured the rest of that water into the coffee kettle, and stirred the fire a bit to heat the iron top. She found the flour, lard, and a bit of milk, and mixed up a pan of biscuits. Then, pulling the cast iron pan into place, she threw in some salt pork Tolbert had left on the table with a scoop of lard. By the time the gravy and eggs were cooked, Tolbert was sitting on the edge of his bed. He watched as the biscuits were pulled from the oven.

"Here's you'ins breakfast," Minnie said.

Tolbert stood and crossed the room, and sat down at the table. Minnie poured him a cup of strong black coffee, and set a plate of food in front of him. Next, she picked up a biscuit, a slice of ham, and a cup of coffee. Then she stepped toward the door, wanting to eat away from him. Tolbert stopped her.

"You'ins not goin to sit and eat, gal? Where you'ins goin in such a hurry?" Tolbert asked with sudden kindness in his voice.

Minnie just stood there with a stunned expression, her mouth hanging open. *Wonder why he bein' so nice*, Minnie thought. "Well," Minnie said, "I wanted to get the seed in the ground 'fore the heat come on. Looks like the sun goin' to be full in the sky today."

"If'in you'ins will slow down, gal, I'll help you'ins."

Minnie nodded, but kept walking out the door, scared she might laugh out loud and get another beating.

"Can you believe this here man? He beats me, drags me like I ain't nothin', and this mornin' his mouth drippin' with honey. What's he *up to?*"

As Minnie was gathering the hoe and seed, she saw Tolbert push the wheel barrel over to the chicken coop. Opening the door and taking a shovel in his hand, he began to remove all the chicken manure and old hay from the coop. As he pushed the overflowing wheel barrel over to the garden site, Minnie began to shake a little, not knowin' what would come next. It didn't make sense.

"If 'in you'in will hand me the rake, I'll rake this manure into the soil, and you come along behind me and make up the rows."

"Uh, okay," said Minnie, confused by his politeness.

A couple of hours passed and the sun was just about nine marks in the sky. With half the rows made, and all the manure spread, Minnie knew by now that something was up. Tolbert was whistling, and she had not seen him take one sip of shine. When he finished with the raking, he even turned that rake up on end, and started helping Minnie cut rows. She took the seeds in her turned-up shirt tail, and slowly, walking down each row, dropped them evenly spaced. Tolbert was right behind her backing up the dirt over the seeds.

Close to dinner time, Tolbert suggested they get some water and a bite to eat.

"I know this might sound like I'm sassin' you'ins but I not. Just want to know why you'in be helpin' me today."

"Well," Tolbert started, "I just thought it's my garden. If'in I want to get some food out of my garden, I better not leave it up to no gal," he said matter-of-factly.

"Now *there*, that's what I s'pect. Not all this honey you been drippin' all morning. Know'd it when I woke up. Something done told me something wasn't right," she grumbled.

"What you mean, gal, *something not right?*"

"Well, you'ins have been mad, a beatin' me since my Paw gave me to you'ins, and all sudden, you'ins just goin' to up and *stop*. Somethin' ain't *right*," she raised her voice.

"*Now gal!*" Tolbert finally snapped. "If'in you'ins want me to beat ya, I can give you'ins a good wallup now, 'cause I ain't listen to no more sass!"

Minnie quickly turned and went back to the garden before she said anything else that would send Tolbert into a fury. *Why can't I learn and keep my mouth shut? I had to go and ruin things. He was tryin' to get along, and there I go running my mouth.*

Minnie watched as Tolbert climbed the steps, and glanced back at her with a half-smile on his face as he walked into the house. A chill went down her spine.

Quickly picking up the seed, Minnie tried to focus on the planting instead of what she feared might happen next. But as she was picking up the hoe to back up the dirt over the seed, a shadow made her start. Looking up, she saw Ishmael.

"Howdy," he smiled. "I never seen a gal work so hard before. Not one 'cept my Maw. You'ins have this farm lookin' better than it ever did before."

"It still got a long way to go. This here just my second day," she sighed, looking away. Compliments were not something Minnie Leigh was accustomed to receiving, so she was slow to respond and, in the end, dropped the hoe and turned on her heel, taking off toward the creek without another word.

Falling next to the stream, Minnie splashed her face with the cool water, wondering what was going on.

She looked up through the trees. "Now God, why you reckon that man there talkin' sweet to me? Matter-of-fact, I don't understand *none* of this here mess. God, I ain't never been churched 'cause my Paw says getting religion was nothin' but a poor man's way to whine about things. But if'in you're real, *help me!* I don't understand why Paw gave me away like I'm one of his cows to be traded, especially to this man here! He's old enough to be a Grandpappy!

"God, I'd leave, but Tolbert 'bout killed me for turnin' around on that path, just to go back and ask my Paw where I was going. 'Sides, I don't have any idey where I'm at, though I figure I could just walk out and start up new wherever I land."

As Minnie walked out of the woods and headed back to the garden, she noticed Tolbert and Ishmael standing by the corral.

Now what you supposin' those two plottin'? Minnie asked herself with narrowed eyes.

Then Tolbert and Ishmael walked up to the edge of the garden. As they did, Ishmael removed his hat, and a slight smile came across his face.

"Hey, gal!" Tolbert yelled.

Startled, and without thinking, Minnie yelled, "Can't you'ins ever use my name? *I have a name!*" as she walked up to them.

"You'ins is real lucky, gal, you belong to Ishmael now, or I would show you'ins a name!" he hollered. Turning to Ishmael, he said, "See what I be talkin' bout? Well, she's your'ins now, good luck."

"What you'ins mean I's his?" Minnie asked.

"Well, you'ins been here two days, and things ain't workin'. You don't know how to cook that good, or make a home, and you lackin' in you'ins other wife duties too," the man shrugged.

"Now you hold on there. That's no way to speak when others are present. She doesn't deserve to be treated like she some animal," Ishmael frowned.

"Why not? She sure been traded enough to be considered one," Tolbert said, letting out a laugh as if someone had just told a joke.

Minnie was furious. "Are you'ins men all crazy? I ain't no livestock to be traded here and yonder! You'ins mens think you'ins own the world. What I get traded for this time? More farmland?"

Tolbert answered with a crooked grin on his face. "I got a mule, a cow, and a good five jugs of shine. Believe me, this here stuff worth more than you *ever* will be."

"Well if that don't skin the cat's hide," she almost rolled her eyes. "Just let me get my things."

Tolbert blocked her. "Things? You'ins ain't *got* no things. Just get to steppin', gal. Follow this here man over the mountain, and don't never come claimin' anything from me or I'll shoot you dead!"

CHAPTER 8

As Minnie was once again ordered to leave with a stranger, her steps didn't feel real. She could see her feet moving, but they looked like the feet of someone else. Numb with disbelief that one person could be tossed from one to another, as if they were of no importance but to satisfy the desire of others, she moved forward, not knowing what she would once again have to endure. Her feet obeyed the commands given to them, to "Move, move along. Hurry, let's get, gal," by her new master.

This time, Minnie didn't record their path in her mind. As if in a dream, she glided through the woods following a figure that was out of focus, knowing, but yet not knowing, that it was all happening again.

Her thoughts were so loud, she didn't know if she was speaking out loud, or if the sound of her voice was coming from inside her head.

"God, you'ins got a real unusual way of loving someone. I don't rightly know what I done to you, but I sure as heck would like to, 'cause this here is something I ain't never heard of. Most folks in these mountains protect their family, and folks they know. Most ever'one I ever come across is right friendly folks. How did it happen to be that you pickin' on *me?*" she spoke quietly to herself.

"What's that you say, gal?" Ishmael asked, turning to look over his shoulder.

"Nothin'," Minnie replied. "I said nothin'."

After an hour and a half walking down a path, they broke into a clearing. Now, if Minnie didn't know better, she would swear she died and went to heaven, for the scene that broke before her was as beautiful as she had ever laid her eyes on. She saw the bright green of grass, a carpet of new growth you only see in early spring, gently waving in the calm breeze that was created from the large waterfall she saw before her. One could imagine that if you stepped on it, you would no longer have to move under your own power. Instead, you'd just float in its swaying.

As she continued to follow Ishmael, they turned left, and before her was one of the prettiest cabins she ever dreamed of seeing.

"Whose place is this?" she asked with wide eyes.

"Why gal, this here is *my* place. I cleared this spot of land when I was a young boy, mostly by myself. It was given to me by my Pappy on my Maw's side when he passed on."

"He sure must love you might strong to have given you all this," Minnie remarked. "Never seen nothin' like it. Well, I saw a waterfall before, but it was always from up to the mountain. Never knew it would be so purty up close," she sighed.

They climbed the steps up onto the porch, where Minnie Leigh dropped into the first chair she saw. Sitting there on the porch, Minnie stared, almost unblinking, toward the falls. She was out of breath from the walk, and numb still with disbelief that just this morning, she was starting to believe in Tolbert because of the way he talked, and because of all the work he'd suddenly put in.

Minnie sat thinking to herself, *After all the hittin' and pain, not to mention all the hard work I was a doin' to make myself a home no matter how bad, I've just been throwed away again. I can't understand what I've done to have been treated so.*

"Now gal, get on up and come in here and start cookin', whiles I go check on my livestock," Ishmael stated, his voice now stern.

Minnie felt as if she was gliding into the house under some power not her own again, and out of some ingrained habit, she started stoking the fire to heat up the stove top. Without much thought, she looked around for something to cook. There was lard, flour, canned vegetables, jars of jelly, and even a bowl of butter. After what seemed to be no time, she had heated beans, and made biscuits and gravy.

After their meal, as Minnie stood over a washtub on the corner of the porch, she saw Ishmael out hoeing in a garden, lost in thought.

"Well, he must not be as terrible as the last one. At least he's out working the garden. Maybe he'll let me go down to town with him. Perhaps I can make extry money diggin' the Ginseng root again."

"Minnie!" Ishmael called as he headed toward the cabin. "Minnie, come here, gal!"

"Yes?" she answered as she turned to face him.

"Let's sit a bit gal, and talk."

"Talk? Why? No one ever wanted to sit and speak to me on purpose before," her eyebrows knitted.

"Yes, talk." Then Ishmael started speaking about his plans for them. Minnie was only half-listening until he started going on about a *real church wedding*, and how many kids they were going to have, hoping they were going to be smart and all.

"I wonder how far Knoxville is from here?"

Not realizing she spoke out loud, she was startled when Ishmael asked, "Why you'ins need to know that? Weren't you listenin' to what I was a saying about the church weddin' and children and makin' a good home for us here? We can start addin' on to the house right away."

"Ishmael, no one asked me what *I* want to do. I don't know you'ins any more than I knew that other man, Tolbert."

"Ain't no one's got to ask you'ins," he told her. "You'ins is a young gal and has no ideas what is best for you'ins. Besides, I done traded fair for you," he nodded.

"You'ins think you'ins knows what is best for me? How havin' a litter of kids all runnin' around good for me? And *traded fair for me?* You'ins think all I's worth is a mule, a cow, and some jugs of moonshine!"

"Well gal, that ain't just any o' shine," Ishmael smiled.

"That there moonshine the best there ever was or ever will be. Not everyone can get their hands on that shine. Now, let me finish what I'm a sayin' bout the church weddin'."

"*What church weddin'?!*" Minnie shouted.

"Now what kinda question is that? I have been tellin' you how I am tryin' to arrange us a real church weddin' so's our children won't be shamed by us not being given to each other by the preacher and all!" he went on.

"Children? *What children?!*" she shouted again.

"Gal, you been livin' long enough now! It's time you'ins start planning your'in first child. I'm takin' you to the healer tomorrow and sees about her fixin' you'ins."

"Fixin' me?! There ain't a thing broke about me!"

"Well, it's about time you have a little one growin' inside you, and you'ins shows no signs. Somethin' has to be wrong with you'ins," he shrugged again, not caring that she was upset.

"Maybe you'ins is the one that needs healin'," Minnie snapped.

"Ain't no man has no troubles plantin' his seed, gal. You'ins women is the ones has a hard time holdin' that seed," he narrowed his eyes.

Minnie was now in full panic. She had to get out of these mountains. She decided she would just go about digging the Ginseng root and keep to herself. All she had to her name was two dollars, which was nothing to be ashamed of, but she knew she would need more.

The next morning was more of the same. She rose early, cooked breakfast, and after the dishes were cleared, she headed outside to the refuge of the woods.

After an hour or so, as Minnie came out of the woods from her early morning dig, Ishmael greeted her.

"Now, what you'in s'pose you got in that their sack, gal? Where you'ins been getting off to evera mornin'?" he raised an eyebrow.

"I have gathered me some Ginseng root, and I's talkin' to

God," Minnie shrugged.

"Talkin' to God? Gal, has you'ins lost your mind?" he shook his head. "Talkin' to God...what do you'ins know about gettin' religion?"

"I don't know nothin' bout it, but that don't stop me from askin' Him questions, does it?"

"Well, I reckon not," Ishmael kept his gaze firm and steady on her to make sure she was not pulling his leg.

Later that evening, the cabin was well lit with kerosene lanterns as they sat at the table for their evening meal. Minnie Leigh was aware that Ishmael had hardly broken his gaze from her since she came back with the Ginseng root and started sewing some clothes. In the close quarters of the small cabin, she began to feel uneasy.

"What all that sewin' and mending going on? I don't see no new shirts or dresses around," Ishmael asked.

"I have just been tryin' to be a good Christian like the preacher be sayin'," she shrugged, not wanting to tell him the truth.

"There you go again. Why you'ins acting like you'ins got religion? I ain't seen you down to the front of the church," he huffed.

"Does that stop me from practicin' so when I get the feelin' of the Holy Ghost to go up to the front, God won't have no reason not to wash me clean and give me religion?" she said quickly.

"Hmmm? If'n you'ins says so. I am just getting' a feelin' that you'ins are up to somthin'," he narrowed his eyes again, not believing her.

"No Ishmael. I ain't up to nothin'."

Minnie started gathering the dishes. She knew now she was going to have to show Ishmael she was an obedient wife. She had to plan how to help herself without getting caught again.

CHAPTER 9

The next day was not unusual, just more of the same clearing trees, milling them into lumber, and hueing logs to add rooms to the cabin. There was also tending livestock, and hoeing in the garden.

Now, Ishmael had left with a few menfolk earlier. "No, tellin' what they all up to," Minnie thought as she worked.

When Ishmael returned, he was impressed with what she had placed on the table. Grabbing for his plate, he piled it full of green beans, and biscuits with gravy on top. With huge bites, and hardly taking a breath, Ishmael ate like he had not eaten in weeks. After sopping up the gravy from his plate, he buttered the biscuits, and spread jelly over them for dessert.

"Now *that* was a meal. I never have food like that unless I visit my Maw," he smiled while patting his belly.

"Wasn't that hard," Minnie said blankly. "Did you can those vegetables and make up that jelly?"

"No," Ishmael laughed. "That's woman's work. My Maw always sends me packin' home with food she done canned. She worries 'cause I don't have no wife. Wait until she meets you'ins. Won't non-my family believe I done caught me a gal as purty and hard workin' as your'in."

Without reply, Minnie cleared the dishes and threw the leftovers out over the porch rail for the dog to eat. It was a chilly night, and going back inside, she pulled a chair next to the stove. Staring blankly, with no real thoughts, she felt empty.

After a while, Ishmael ordered Minnie to go to bed, and just as if she was under that power other than her own again, she walked over and laid down on the bed. She only drifted off to sleep after what seemed to be half the night.

Sometime early in the morning, she was awakened by Ishmael laying on top of her, the foul smell of shine on his breath, pulling at her clothes. Her heart racing, she began to hit and scream, and with a force that seemed to come from someone much stronger, she pushed him to the floor and managed to escape.

Minnie flew out of the cabin, and ran through the woods. Not knowing where she was going, or caring, she ran until she could run no more.

Finally, she stopped and leaned against a tree trunk where she began to cry. The tears would not stop, and her heart felt as if it would bust right out of her chest if she cried any harder.

Then the dawn began to break. Pushing herself to her feet, she started walking, nowhere in particular, just away from what seemed to be a bad dream. But with every ache of her heart, and tears that would not stop, she knew it had all been real. She walked some more, stopping only for water.

Minnie paused to rest, what she summed up to be just after the noon sun. She gathered her thoughts, pulled herself upright, and for the first time in weeks, she made a decision for herself.

"I'll get out of these mountains just like momma did. I'll explore what's on that road down yonder. Can't be no worse than what I been given here." With steps of her own choosing this time, she made her way on through the woods.

After what seemed like no time, she heard children laughing. Following the sounds, she soon saw where the commotion was coming from. She saw children running in and out of blankets that hung on a line out in the sun, and one of the children stopped to greet her as she came closer.

"What you'ins name?" she asked.

Bending down, she said, "Why, I'm Minnie Leigh Robertson. Who mightin' you'ins be?"

Before the child could answer, there stood a woman with hands on her hips looking like an old mother bear raised up to protect her cubs.

"Lucy!" the mother said sternly, pointing to the ground next to her. Without hesitation, the child ran to stand next to her. "What you a doin', gal? Where you'ins come from?"

"Well ma'am, I just thought I'd get down this mountain and see what I could find."

"Where's your'in Maw and Paw?" the woman asked.

"Don't have none left, I be on my own," Minnie said as a shiver ran down her back from the lie she just told.

"Well, I don't know if'n I'd go down to the valley without no man folk," the woman raised an eyebrow.

"I done told you, I don't have no one," Minnie just sighed. "Just lookin' for somewhere different to see what else there is," she added with all the confidence in her voice she could find.

"Well get you a drink of water out that well over yonder, then be on your way," the mother remarked with a single nod. As she walked away toward the cabin, she gathered her children.

Minnie Leigh ran to the well and dropped the bucket down the shaft. Then turning the handle, she drew up a bucket full of clear, cold water. Taking the ladle from the nail where it hung beneath the roof built over the well, she drank what seemed to be a bucket full. Then she wet her shirttail, and washed her face.

"Hey, gal."

Frightened by the break in the silence, Minnie spun on her heels, only to see the mother standing in front of her. Stretching her arm out, the woman handed Minnie a napkin filled with biscuits and a couple of slices of meat.

"Thank ya ma'am, I was getting a bit hungry," Minnie nodded gratefully.

Pointing to a path, the woman explained to Minnie that she should follow that path until it came to the wagon trail, and follow the trail toward the sun. This trail would take her to the bottom of the mountain where she would find another road. "Where you go from there is up to you'ins." Then turning, she walked away.

Full of fear and excitement, Minnie headed down the path onto the trail that descended by winding one way, then another.

Just before dusk, Minnie came to the end of the trail, and she knew she was in the bottomland because she had never seen such a wide-open area except from her mountain top.

CHAPTER 10

Minnie Leigh walked as far as she could before dusk arrived, giving herself enough time to gather wood for a fire, and dry leaves and pine straw to make a place to bed down for the night. Though her legs ached from the great distance she had covered in a day, she felt light-hearted, and just knew she could keep going no matter how long it took.

After finding an area with thick brush cover well off the side of the road, Minnie built up a fire. Using dry pine straw she had gathered, she made a soft bed under the brush to protect her from early morning dew. Minnie Leigh found herself grateful for knowing mountain ways. She knew deep in her soul that they would help her survive.

The next morning, she woke just as dawn began to break. Without starting a fire, she went to a nearby stream, and washed her face. Without pausing, she stood, made her way back to the road, and continued to walk.

As the sun began to climb to mid-morning, Minnie felt her bones warm, and for the first time in weeks, she felt a bit calm and relaxed.

"Good morning sun, good morning world. Good morning God, it's Minnie Leigh. This here bottomland is as beautiful close up as it was from my mountain. Everything's bigger than I thought it was, though. I always wondered why there were patches of brown in the mist of the green valley. Now I see it's only where the corn has dried, or Tobacco has been cut. I don't know where I'm going, but I s'pect you'll help me. That if'n you'ins done with trading me around. I s'pose I find me some vittles somewhere. Hopefully soon, my stomach about to gnaw right through my skin."

Minnie continued to walk along the road, and though she had seen cabins and houses here and there, she hadn't laid eyes on one person. She knew there were people around. She could see the smoke from chimneys, and cattle and livestock in fenced corrals and fields.

After a short time, she heard a noise. It was familiar, but she could not place it. Then suddenly, her question was answered by a vehicle of some kind passing her.

"Well, I'll be. Never seen a vehicle that looks like that," she said out loud. Only then did Minnie realize she was talking to herself. She laughed. "I'm touched, of course, what else? Better stop this jabbering 'fore someone chains me to a tree out in the woods."

Walking along, she remembered she had about a half a biscuit and a sliver of meat left that she had stuffed in her pocket earlier. But as Minnie pulled the kerchief from her pocket, crumbs fell to the ground. The biscuit reduced to fine crumbs, with just enough meat to give her a taste. With her fingers and thumb, she pinched up the crumbs, and placed them in her mouth.

Now that was only enough to make me hungrier. Better than nothin' I s'pose. I'll have to stop early enough to see about making me a trap to catch a rabbit, squirrel, something, she thought, the hunger making her feel more and more tired as she walked on.

Tears begin to form in Minnie's eyes for the first time since yesterday morning, when she took her first steps onto the mountain road. Her mind and emotions were all over the place as she began to think that her Paw traded her like she never mattered to him. The tears became more substantial as she thought of Tolbert, and how from the start, he hit her, then later raped her, doing it all under the rights of a man.

"What did I ever do to be treated so bad? Lord, help me!"

Minnie did not realize the grass had ended, and she had stepped into a large area that had been beat down to dirt where wagons, cars, and trucks had repeatedly entered and parked. She merely collapsed from her reeling emotions, tears, and exhaustion. She sat there crying uncontrollably, and laid down right there, unable to pick herself up.

"Come on, dear. It'll be ok. Get up, come with me."

Minnie Leigh was startled and frightened that Ishmael, or worse, Tolbert, had found her. She pulled her hand from the one that had taken hers. But as she looked up and focused on the face above her, she saw a lady looking at her with concern. Minnie stuck her hand back out, and accepted the help that was offered.

"There now dear one, you just come with me. First, let's get you washed up. You look like you could use some food."

"Could I!" Minnie cried with excitement. "I ain't had no real vittles since I left—" But Minnie stopped herself. She didn't want anyone knowing where she was from. *I can't take a chance, they might return me to the menfolk*, she thought, *and I'm not going back.*

"You know gal, when I first saw you out here, I thought you were some young boy hitchin' to Knoxville. I didn't 'spec' you were female in those clothes. I know you're not from around here. I know all the locals. Where did you come from?"

"I come from nowhere," Minnie answered quickly.

"Nowhere? Okay, *gal from nowhere*. Let's get you washed up, and then get you something to eat."

"I sure could use some vittles. That be mighty kind."

Minnie followed her new acquaintance into a road side café. Walking in, Minnie noticed chairs at a long bar. Behind it were all kinds of machines like nothing she had ever seen before. Tables with checkered table clothes and four chairs at each table sat in various areas around the room. The aroma of food cooking smelled heavenly, and Minnie Leigh realized just how hungry she was. For the better part of two days, she had walked along the strange road, not knowing where it would take her. All Minnie knew was that she was free of all those that seemed to want to bring her nothing but harm.

She followed the stranger into the room to a back door.

Outside the door was a table that held a pitcher and face bowl, just like she had used at home. The lady took the pitcher, walked over to a pipe sticking up out of the ground, and turned a knob. Water came pouring out.

"*Lord of mercy*, where all that water spilling from? How you did that?"

"Why girl, it's just a water faucet."

"Water *what?*" Minnie raised an eyebrow.

"Now I *know* you're not from here. You sound like you been hid out from the world, and the only place I know like that anywhere around here, is up *there.*"

As the lady pointed to the mountain in the distance, Minnie became frightened once again of being returned to the life she'd just left.

"Don't be so skittish girl, I'm not going to tell your secret. At least not until I know your story."

"My story? Well, I don't have no story," Minnie raised her eyebrow even higher.

"Girl, we all have a story. I have a story. Your story is just where you come from, what your life has been, and looking at you, I'd say yours has been a troublesome one."

"Troublesome? You got that part right. Least, that's a nice way of puttin' it," Minnie huffed tiredly.

"Well, whatever it is can wait. Here now, get washed up while I go and see if I can fetch you some clean clothes."

Minnie did as she was told. When the stranger returned, she was carrying a bright colored dress and a pair of short bloomers, along with a funny looking thing with two cups and straps.

Pointing to the odd piece of clothing, Minnie asked, "What kind of clothes is that?"

"Why girl, haven't you ever seen a brazier before?"

"A what?"

"Come with me, I'll explain it," the lady smiled.

Minnie followed the lady through a door into a room that jutted out from the back of the building. As they entered, Minnie saw a small bed, and a chest of draws. As they walked into the room, the lady bent over, and with a clicking sound, the room lit up.

"You didn't need a match for the lantern. How did you *do* that? This here's the strangest place I ever knew. Water's coming out the ground without a pale or a pump, and now a lantern that needs no matches!"

"You know, I've forgotten all my manners. My name's Betty. You can call me Miss Betty; and may I know your name?"

"My name be Minnie Leigh Robertson."

"Your name *be?* I take you never been to school and learned how to speak proper English."

"What's English?" Minnie blinked in more confusion.

Laughing, Miss Betty just shook her head. "Come on, we'll worry about that later. Let me show you how to use a brazier, and then you can dress. Once you're dressed, just come back inside and have a bite to eat."

Betty showed Minnie how to put a brazier on, which didn't make much sense. It wasn't comfortable at all.

But the dress was soft and bright yellow, with small flowers all over it. It reminded Minnie of the hillside back home, like the sun when it was shining down a patch of Brown-Eyed Susans. Minnie pulled the dress over her head, though never having one of her own, her legs felt naked, and she was embarrassed to go inside. There had been some menfolk sitting at one of the tables. As she entered, she felt their eye fall on her, and without hesitation, the young one let out a whistle.

"You sure clean up mighty fine there, little lady. Why don't you come over here and sit a spell with us?"

Minnie ducked her head a little, and gazed at the floor frozen in her steps.

"Now you going to act shy and innocent. You don't *look* like no innocent girl to me."

"You stop that right now, young man!" Betty yelled across the room. "I won't have you ogling this young lady."

"I ain't ogling nobody, just tryin' to be friendly to the new

54

girl," he snickered.

"You don't worry about being nice to the new girl. She doesn't have any interest in you or anyone else."

"Who you to tell me what I can do, Betty? You sure is a sassy thing. Maybe I should be ogling *you*."

"Ogle me, and you'll be wearing one of my cast iron skillets across that big ol' head of yours!" she threatened.

The young man became silent and angry as his friends at the table around him began to snicker and laugh one by one.

Minnie walked on around the long, high counter, and Betty held a plate of food in her hand as she pointed to a table well away from prying eyes. Minnie sat down, and grabbing up the spoon in her fist that was lying next to the plate, she began to shovel the food in her mouth without so much as taking a breath. Betty, laying her hand on Minnie's said, "Slow down, Minnie. There's no need to hurry. Take your time. Here, take a drink of cold milk. Wash that mouth full of food down."

"I'm so hungry, I don't want to slow down," Minnie said between bites.

"Well, you'll choke if you don't slow down some. The food isn't going anywhere, and there's no one here to take it from you."

Minnie finished off the plate of food, not caring what it was that she was eating, only that it was hot and filling. Next, Betty brought her a saucer with a slice of apple pie on it. That too disappeared in record time.

Minnie hadn't noticed the time, but the sun began to set, and the room began to clear of the few people that had come in while she was eating. As the last one left, Betty stepped to the door, turned on a sign that was hanging on the outside, closed the door, locked it, and pulled the shade down. She hurried to each window, pulling shades. Betty came over to where Minnie was sitting, and took a seat opposite her.

"Now Minnie, I don't know where you came from or where you thought you were going all by yourself down this long road. Wherever you come from, you seemed mighty frightened to go back. But you have no worries here. No one will send you back, and you don't have to worry about whatever or whoever it is you're so frightened of."

"Okay," Minnie answered. "I was wonderin', could I stay tonight and sleep in that bed I saw in that back room? I slept on the ground last night, and my bones are achin'. A bed would sure feel good."

"Well girl, did you think I was going to put you out on the ground after giving you those clean clothes and feeding you? No, you'll sleep here tonight, in a bed, and in the morning, we'll decide what's next."

Without argument or another word, Minnie stood and walked to the back room, and shut the door. She walked to the bed, pulling the covers down as she climbed in. She was asleep before her head touched the pillow.

CHAPTER 11

When Minnie opened her eyes, she rose, confused by her surroundings. She didn't recognize anything that laid before her as she sat on the side of the bed. Things came into focus as her head cleared of sleep, and she remembered where she was. She stood and walked to the door. It was early morning, but the sun had not begun to peak over the horizon. Minnie looked around for an outhouse, but in the pitch black, she couldn't see any further than the light that spilled from her room. Stepping down to the ground from the steps, the ground was cold to her bare feet.

"Well, I can't wait," Minnie placed her hand on the side of the building, and followed it to the end. She then squatted, pulled down her bloomers, and relieved her bladder right there on the ground. Then she walked to the door that led into the café.

She could see a sliver of light around the edge of the shade, so she tried the knob. It was open, though before going in, she splashed her face and washed her hands in the face bowl which remained on the table next to the door. Entering, she walked around the long bar to find Betty sitting at a table drinking coffee and writing in a book.

Looking up, Betty greeted Minnie. "Good morning. I thought you would be sleeping at least to sun up this morning. Did you rest well? Did you find the shower house okay?"

"I slept like a bear tuck up for the winter," Minnie admitted. "What's a shower house?"

"It's an indoor outhouse, and a shower is running water

that sprays over you so that you can clean yourself."

Betty smiled, almost laughed at the innocent, but matter-of-fact way Minnie answered everything. She didn't know it yet, but these matter-of-fact answers and questions would become a familiar chatter in her café.

"Do you sleep in here?" Minnie asked.

"Why, no girl. I have a cabin out back, a home," Betty explained.

"Where's your man?"

"My man?"

"Yea, your husband. Doesn't he work with you?"

"No Minnie, I don't have a husband, and everyone that works here works for me. I own this place," she smiled.

"You own this? How can you own this without a man?"

"Minnie, you don't have to have a man to own something."

"That's not what I been told," Minnie huffed.

"Well, you been told wrong. I was married when I was younger, but my husband got himself killed in Knoxville. I found this land and needed to make some money. All I knew how to do is cook and clean, so I copied the café I'd eaten at in Knoxville, then added a few small cabins on the other side of the building. I feed travelers and sometimes locals, and I let the cabins out to those who need to rest from a long ride between Johnson City and Knoxville. Occasionally, I get someone from Chicago, and even New York.

"Now, Bean Station is no Johnson City or Chicago. It's not even near the size of Knoxville, but there are times you would think it is. All those fancy folks are coming to Tate Springs paying for mineral water. They come by the train-car load to feel better. I say they come to clear their lungs of city dirt, and their heads of the noise."

"I know where Johnson City is, and I've been told about Chicago, but never heard of Tate Springs. It sounds like you pullin' my leg. Why would anyone pay for water when all you have to do is take a bucket down to the creek and draw it up?

Or get themselves one of those fancy pipes coming up out of the ground like you have?" Minnie asked with a laugh.

"You have no idea of all the things you have to discover, things that make life a little easier, things mountain folk still have no idea even exist. How does a young girl from the mountaintop know about Chicago, but you've never seen an electric light or even a water faucet?"

"My Paw's a shiner. Sometimes I'd come down the mountain with him to unload a big order of shine, and there'd be these men there in fancy suits and hats. My Paw said they was from a town called Chicago."

"Chicago hasn't been a town for a long time. Chicago's a vast city with houses built right next to each other, and so many people you can hardly breathe. New York's the same, but much bigger."

"Why would you build a cabin right next to your neighbors with so much land?"

"Well Minnie, in a city, even one as small as Knoxville, most people can only afford to let a single room, one of many in a single building. Some of those buildings have up to two hundred rooms."

"You're joshin' me now," Minnie shook her head. "It'd take a building bigger than a barn to put two hundred rooms in it."

"Minnie, you sure have a lot to learn, and a lot of surprises in store for you," Betty started to explain. "Buildings are built up, not out like a barn. Maybe one day, you'll make it to Knoxville and you'll see. Here and there, there are cities as old as our country. City people would be as surprised as you are if they came here that there's so much land free of traffic and noise. These families go way back. Their ancestors came over here when America was young. They lived and worked in the first town they landed in. Some stayed to earn money to buy land. Others came with money they had saved and just moved on.

"The towns grew larger. Before you knew it, an open plot of land was filled with stores and houses and factories. Families grew and expanded and never left, generation after generation."

"It's the same where I come from. Families have been planted there from the beginning of time. Paw told me. He's the one that told me about how big the world was. He went on a boat across the ocean. He told me the ocean is like a million lakes put together. He said it can get very angry though, when a storm passes through, so angry that it tries to sink the ships tossing them around and up and down. He said there was nothing for me to see, that we had all we need, and there was nowhere in the world as good as living in the mountains."

"He must've been in the Great War."

"I think that's what he called it. He was gone a long time, so long my mom up and left. Just got up one day, walked into the woods, and never heard from her again. Now I don't remember her. I was just a babe of three when she left. Paw told me about her. He would sometimes become very angry with me cause my Maw didn't take me with her."

"Why would he be angry with you? You were just a small child. You could not choose to stay or go," Betty stated, her expression soft.

"I know, but he would get angry just the same," Minnie shrugged.

"What kind of work does your father do again?"

"Work? Well, my Paw doesn't do much work at all. He sells moonshine. Then when he runs out, and we need supplies, he'll make a batch, sell it, and then fetch a wagon of goods from the local mercantile."

"*Mercantile?* Now, there's a word I haven't heard in a while," Better laughed lightly. Then she thought of something. "Minnie, I have an idea I'd like to present to you. You want to hear it?"

"What kind of idea? Lately, other folk's ideas haven't been too good to me," Minnie drew her lips into a tight, nervous line.

"Well, let me tell you mine, and if you think it would not help you, then okay. You decide."

"You goin' to let me decide?" Minnie raised an eyebrow.

"Well sure I am. You're getting to be a young lady, and

you'll have to be able to make decisions. That is, until you get married."

"Oh *no!* I ain't never getting married again," Minnie huffed loudly.

"Again? What do you mean *again?* You're not old enough to have been anyone's wife yet," Betty remarked with confusion.

"Believe me, I've been married, and I'm not having no man hit me, drag me by my hair, or anything else ever! *No ma'am*, not this girl!" Minnie's began to raise her voice, her breathing speeding up.

"That's not what marriage is about, Minnie. That's not how it is at all," Betty reassured her calmly.

But Minnie wasn't hearing it. "I've been married twice in the last few weeks, I know what marriage is," she snapped.

"Twice in a few weeks? I don't understand. But we'll just let it go for now, the subject has you all upset," Betty frowned, figuring it was better to let the girl talk when she felt like it.

"Good. Now, which way to Knoxville? I'll need to be heading out 'fore it gets late," the girl announced.

"Thought you were going to listen to my idea before you made any decisions," the woman reminded Minnie patiently.

"Okay, let's hear it," Minnie crossed her arms, waiting impatiently.

"Well, I thought you could stay here for a while. See, I lived in Knoxville, and a lady needs to know how to take care of herself if she's no longer married," Betty said this with a slight smile on her face. Just the thought of a young girl telling such tales. "My idea is, I would teach you how to work here, and you could go to school for a while. Do you know how to read and write?"

"I'm not stupid, my Paw learned me to write my name. But I'm not much on reading, so don't think I'll need to learn that."

"Believe me, Minnie, there're a lot of things you should learn if you plan on living in Knoxville. You'll need to know these things to get a good job, one that's suited for a young lady."

"I'll think about it," Minnie shrugged again. "I don't know if I need all that. I'm a strong girl and I work very hard. I know how to find the best herbs and Ginseng there is. I make good money when I sell it. I can build a strong fence, milk cows, make butter, can vegetables."

"Minnie, even though those are very admirable things, there's not much call for them in the city. You'll need to learn something new to survive," Betty shook her head.

"If'n you say so. Like I said, I'd think on it. May I have some coffee and some breakfast? I need to get outside, greet the day."

"Sure. Minnie, come around here, I'll show you how to make coffee," Betty let the topic go for now.

"See, I know how to make coffee already and cook."

"Oh, do you? Well, I think my coffee kettle is different from what you use at home. Other than that, I'm sure you can handle it," Betty said, knowing better. "My stove works differently from yours too, we have a gas stove. These machines here on the counter run off electricity. You know how I lit the lantern without a match in your room? The reason I can do that is it has electricity."

"That reminds me, I couldn't get it to go out when I went to bed. I let it burn all night."

"Don't worry Minnie, I'll show you how things work. This is the very reason I want you to stay a while. If you went to Knoxville, there're so many things you couldn't do just because you don't understand how modern things work."

"Told you I'd think about it," the girl sighed.

Betty would not admit it to herself, but Minnie gave her a daughter, a child if only for a short time, a child longed for but never realized. The day was spent going from waiting on customers to showing Minnie how to work the equipment in the café.

The cook, a middle-aged black lady, was eager to help her learn how to work the stove. She was excited to share her knowledge with someone else, especially someone so keen on learning.

After a week or two, Betty decided it was time for Minnie to be introduced to the teacher and students at the local schoolhouse.

Now, Bean station was a prominent little town, but the population was not very large. Most students in this area were not able to finish school. In the fall, there was harvesting and planting winter crops, killing of the hogs, and molasses to be made. Winter snows also prevented a lot of them making it to the school. Any student who wished to go to school beyond the eighth grade had to board in one of the large towns. The small population did not warrant hiring and paying a teacher for higher learning.

Minnie had never ridden in a motor vehicle, and it was quite a thrill as she and Betty drove the few miles to meet with the teacher. School hadn't started the new term yet, so it was a good time for Minnie to get acquainted with her teacher, Miss Maple. Though Minnie had never been a shy person, she was nervous walking up to the little school house.

Entering the large open room, there were ten rows of desks. In the front left corner, there was a pot belly stove for heat. However, today the tall windows were open, letting in a breeze that cooled the large room.

"Miss Maple, my name is Betty Jefferson. I own the *Roadside Café* and cabins off of Highway Eleven."

"Hello," Ms. Maple smiled.

"This is Minnie Leigh Robertson. She'll be staying with me for a while, so we thought we would come over and find out about the upcoming school term."

"I'll be glad to answer any questions you have. Minnie, what grade level have you completed?" the teacher asked.

"I ain't never been schooled before."

"I see. So, you'd have to start with the lower level children and work your way through to higher grades," Ms. Maple nodded.

"I can write my name. I never learned to read. There not much I need reading for, never had books around."

"If you can write your name, you can learn to read. Reading is used for a lot of things, Minnie, not just to read books. You need it to read the menu at the café so that you can help the customers. You'll need to know how to read the departure board at a train station. Trust me, you will soon realize how much reading will help you."

"Like I told Miss Betty, I would think about it," Minnie shrugged.

"Thank you, Miss Maple, for your time. We'll let you know what Minnie decides."

"No need. If she decides to attend school, all she has to do is show up the first day of school."

The ride back to the café was quiet. Minnie Leigh was watching the landscape.

The more she stared, the more the mountain she used to call home seemed to be getting larger, and reached out to grab her. Minnie shrank in the car seat, squeezing her eyes closed. She was hoping that it would make the mountain go away.

"Minnie, are you okay?" Betty asked.

"Yes, I'm okay. Just got sick to my stomach," she grumbled.

"I'm sure it's because you've never been in a motor car before. It moves faster than a wagon. It's not unusual," the woman didn't push.

Worried that somehow Tolbert or Ishmael would find her if she looked too long at the mountain, Minnie kept her eyes closed until Betty stopped the car in front of the café.

CHAPTER 12

Over the next month and a half, Minnie learned how to wait for the tables in the café with a smile, and running the electric equipment behind the counter was becoming easier. Electricity and running water were becoming second nature; however, she still marveled how much time she saved in a day just from those two things. Even building a fire in a stove with embers sometimes took a while. A meal couldn't be cooked until the iron top heated. With a gas stove, food could cook much faster. No cutting a tree down, sawing into sections to be split, not to mention keeping it stacked high enough to make sure supplies were not depleted in bad weather. Running water was instant. At home, it would take quite a few pulls from the well, lowering the bucket over and over just to have enough water to cook a meal, and then clean the dishes. Reminiscing, Minnie thought how many times she chose to bathe in the ice-cold rivers and streams, just to keep from drawing water over and over, then heating it on the stove top just to wash.

The only challenge that remained was reading and writing. Minnie had a keen mind though. She was able to take orders for a four-top table without writing it down, and repeat them to the cook. Rarely did she get it wrong. Friendly banter with the regular customers became something she looked forward to. Minnie learned very quickly if you treated your customers well, they would leave you a little extra change on the table. The quart-sized mason jar under her bed was almost full.

"I'll be rich before I ever get to Knoxville. I'll not have to live in one of those tiny rooms. Why, I must have about thirty dollars saved already."

Before she knew it, it was time to start school. But the thought of going to the schoolhouse didn't worry her any longer. She'd become aquatinted with the neighbors, and even made a couple of friends. With the town being rather small, one could learn everyone around by either attending church or working in the café as she did. Betty taught her how to help support the community just by making good choices. The vegetables, meat, milk, and butter were all bought from local farmers.

Betty had told Minnie Leigh how she'd planned to make a good profit with her little business by growing all her supplies, raising a beef cow, fatting her hog. But once the café opened, and Betty began to become acquainted with folks, she quickly saw that she was not the only one trying to survive and make a living. Once she started trading and buying the various items needed for the café more, more locals came with their boxes of fresh foods, eggs, milk, even soap for washing dishes. They became family, and they depended on one another to strengthen their homes and town.

The one thing Minnie realized one day was the menfolk were never drunk from shine. It made her feel safe, somehow protected.

"Betty, one thing I sure don't miss is Paw and his friends gather up outside drinkin' and swearin'. There was always a fight, and several times, one or the other would be cut up bad, they'd almost die right outside the cabin."

"No, Minnie," Betty shook her head. "It's against the law to have liquor, or sell it. Don't get me wrong, there're those that travel over to that mountain of yours and brings a truckload back with them. If they ever get caught, the revenue man will lock them up. What made you think of that?"

"I don't know. Once in a while my mind goes back to the mountain and I remember how it was there," she shrugged.

"Are you homesick, Minnie? Do you want to go back or maybe go visit your Pa?" Betty began to suggest.

But Minnie shook her head hard. "Lawd, no! I don't ever want to see him again. He traded me like I was *livestock*. I don't want to see him at all. And them two husbands of mine, I'd be scared they would find me up there. Naw thank you'ins!"

"Whew girl, that mountain talk sure comes out of you when you get fired up," the woman smiled, not really paying any mind to Minnie talking about her *husbands* again.

"You'ins mean I sound like bottomland people now?"

"No, your mountain talk gets thick when you get angry. Going to school will help you learn more about speaking properly. Speaking of school, do you have your things together that Miss Maple said you would need?"

"Yes ma'am," Minnie said. "My dress is laid out, and my slate, chalk, and box for my vittles are ready. You think Sadie will be there?"

"Why, sure. This's her last year of schooling. I don't think she'd miss it."

"Her last year? She my age," the girl blinked in confusion.

"Yes, Minnie. But she's been attending school since she was a young girl. I wouldn't worry if I was you, though. You're a very smart girl. I wouldn't be surprised if you finished in one term." Betty felt this was not entirely true, but why not send Minnie off full of confidence in her ability to learn anything she wanted?

Betty watched as Minnie glided from table to table talking with customers. She'd come accustomed to them laughing at the simplest of her speech and tall tales she would spin.

Minnie was blossoming into a beautiful young lady. Her strawberry blonde hair pulled back with a scarf was no longer covered by a ratty old hat. It was a joy to see. Betty had often questioned if she'd done the right thing building and opening this café with its roadside cabins, but watching Minnie Leigh, she would never question herself about it again. If she hadn't built this place, Minnie would've been in Knoxville, and there was no telling what would've happened to her. With her naïve manner and trusting nature, not to mention no education,

Betty shivered to think about it.

They both woke the next morning with a nervous expectation. Minnie had insisted that she would walk the four miles to the schoolhouse. Betty wasn't keen on the idea, but knew Minnie Leigh had an innate need to be slightly independent. So, she gave in.

Minnie was up before the sun, dressed and in the café with the coffee going, when Betty entered the back door.

"What're you doing up so early? Schoolhouse bell doesn't ring until seven."

"My sleep was fretful. I don't know what's wrong with me," Minnie explained matter-of-factly.

"You'll be ok," Betty just smiled. "First day jitters."

"*Jitters?* Ha," Minnie laughed a deep laugh. "Miss Betty, you can say some of the funniest things I ever heard of."

It was Betty's turn to laugh. "That's like the pot calling the kettle black. You think I can come up with some funny sayings?"

"Me? I ain't never said nothin' like *jitters*," the girl said with a chuckle.

"No? What you think you'in and your'ins sound like to us bottomland folks? *Quit goin' around your butt to get to your elbow.* Better yet, *She's so ugly, her face would turn sweet milk to clabber.* Then there is, *I fixin' to fix.* Some of the funniest things said in this café come out of that sweet mouth of yours," Betty's voice grew soft as she spoke. "I wouldn't have it any other way though. I love that rhythmic speech of yours, especially when you get to really talking to someone you're comfortable around. Never lose that, Minnie."

"Well, maybe I'll learn all that fancy stuff at that schoolhouse," Minnie shrugged, but she was smiling too.

"I hope so, Minnie. I hope so."

Every day, Betty found herself more and more at ease with Minnie around, and she became a little teary-eyed while standing over the stove cooking up some eggs and toasted bread for Minnie and herself. They remained quiet through breakfast, each deep in their own thoughts. Peace laid over both, a peace neither had experienced before. About a quarter-to-six AM, Minnie stood, and picked up her slate and tin box that held her lunch.

"Well, I'm going to head out. I don't want to be late for my first day."

"You sure you need to leave so early?" Betty grew hopeful.

"Not sure, so's I'm goin' to go ahead and leave. I don't walk that fast, ya knows."

"Yes, I do know that," the woman sighed, but understood. "Don't you stop for nothing. Go straight on to school." Still, she tried once more. "If you want to stay a little longer, I can drive you over there."

"I ain't no sissy girl that needs to be carted everywhere. I can walk," she shrugged, not catching Betty's intention. 'Sides, I can greet the mornin' as I walk."

"Okay Minnie, have a good day. Don't worry if you have a little trouble with the lesson today. Remember, schooling is something you never experienced before." Betty wanted to re-assure Minnie any way she could.

"Well, it ain't like I's goin' to my grave or nothin'," Minnie huffed.

With that, Minnie Leigh was out the door, and down the road. As she walked along, she greeted the morning, which she had done every morning since she could remember.

"Good mornin', big ole sky. Come on, you big, old sun. Get on up a bit so's I can see the dew diamonds b'fore I go inside for the day," Minnie nodded, then sighed. "God, I have somethin' I need to say to you, and I hopes you listen to me. I want to just be a sayin' I'm powerful sorry for getting mad at you all those times when I accused you of not bein' real 'cause things was bad. Well, the ways I feelin' this mornin', I don't speck I'll never doubt you again.

"Now, when I was comin' down that road some long weeks back, it had to be you that pushed me down to the ground right there in front of Miss Betty's café. Never had a Maw, but I'm thinkin' if I did, she would be a lot like Miss Betty. So's, I want to thank you for a bring me this way."

Minnie continued to talk and greet the morning, and what seemed like no time passed as she came to the narrow road that leads up to the schoolhouse. The grounds and building were empty, not a soul in sight, so Minnie took a seat on the steps and waited. After a short time, a vehicle topped the little hill, and came to a stop right in front of the steps. Minnie didn't recognize the man driving; however, but he'd sure seen her around, and there was a short hello.

The two boys climbed out of the opposite side, and came around and stood at the foot of the steps. As the man backed his vehicle up, Minnie noticed he hadn't taken his eye off her. It gave her a shiver up her spine, and she made a note in her mind to never see him again if she could.

"You must be that crazy girl that's livin' over at Miss Betty's Roadside," the oldest boy suddenly said.

"I don't be knowin' of no crazy girl at Miss Betty's, but I do live there," Minnie answered, raising an eyebrow.

They both laughed *"You don't be knowin'?* Now, what kind of talk is that? You sound like you might be touched, girl."

Just as Minnie started to stand to fight both of them, an older truck pulled up beside the building. Both boys took off toward the truck., and after a minute, she saw why. It was Miss Maple. The boys were carrying some books for her.

Minnie stepped down from the steps and greeted her teacher. She noticed a group of kids walking over toward them, but she hadn't seen Sadie yet, and began to get a little nervous. She'd been acquainted with a couple of the others, but not like Sadie. They'd become fast friends.

As Miss Maple walked toward the tall post that supported the bell, Minnie finally saw Sadie come up over the hill on horseback, her brother propped behind her. He was a few years younger than Minnie and Sadie. They'd all become close over the last month, scouting the woods as Minnie taught them about herbs and Ginseng and told them tales from the mountain. Minnie greeted them, and they entered the schoolhouse together just as Miss Maple finished ringing the bell.

Everyone was sitting quietly in their seats waiting for Miss Maple. Minnie sat in the desk Sadie pointed out to her.

"Good morning, class."

"G-o-o-d m-o-r-n-i-n-i-n-g M-i-s-s M-a-p-l-e," the class spelled in unison. Minnie just looked around at everyone, puzzled to the slow, mournful way they greeted their teacher.

"Sadie, I'd like you to come up and read our scripture for us this morning. Jake, you come on up, and you'll lead us in the pledge to our Flag." Jake was the older boy that had made fun of the way Minnie spoke, and Minnie could feel herself getting angry as she watched him walk to the front of the class.

"Minnie, I know this is all strange for you. Follow along the best you can this morning. I'll have Sadie go over a few things with you later today."

Minnie raised her hand to her face because all of a sudden, she felt like she had a high fever. But as Sadie began to read, and the pledge was sited, she noticed the warmth left as quickly as it had come.

Now, what you s'pose I getting', a fever for? I'll have to tell Miss Betty I ain't never felt such a heat rise so fast.

And so, began Minnie's first day of school. Miss Maple moved her to the front of the class with the younger students, which caused much laughter from all the other kids except for Sadie and her brother. Sadie scolded everyone before she thought twice. It embarrassed her, and made her very uncomfortable for her friend. Miss Maple hushed the class.

Lunch came and went. The afternoon was spent with Sadie and Minnie sitting on the school house steps as Sadie explained in short form about why they said a pledge to the flag. She also helped Minnie struggle through the beginner reader that Miss Maple had given her. Just like had been predicted, she was learning to read her first day, though the pronunciation of the letters was slow as she struggled to put the sounds together.

The first day ended. Minnie, Sadie, and Scotty left together, Sadie and Scotty on horseback, and Minnie walking beside them.

"What're you so quiet for, Minnie?" Sadie asked.

"Just thinkin' how hard learnin' is. I'm plum tuckered out."

"I sure like the way you talk sometimes," Scotty said with a shy smile on his face.

"Why, thank ya, Scotty. That there one of the nicest things I did heard today."

Sadie and Scotty let out a soft giggle at their friend's strange way of expressing herself.

Betty was sitting on a bar stool she'd pulled up next to one of the front windows, biting her nails and anxious to find out how Minnie's day had gone.

"Miss Betty, you hankerin' for that gal. She'll come through that door soon 'nuff," said the cook from the service window. "I done fixed her a plate of vittles back here. A grown gal can't last all day 'til evenin' time for proper nurshin'."

"Thank you, Lilly Mae. She probably will need something to eat." As Betty turned back and looked through the window, Minnie Leigh was crossing the dirt lot toward the door. Quickly, Betty jumped up and put the stool in its place at the bar, took the dish towel from her pocket, and began wiping down the nearest tabletop. Minnie came through the front door, and walked straight through the back and out to her room, Betty and Lilly Mae staring after her with concern. Betty went running toward the back door, but stopped short.

"No, no. I can't do that, I have to let her come to me if she's upset. She has to learn to live with people."

However, Betty couldn't stop herself from pacing with concern. Minnie had quickly found her way into Betty's heart, and Betty found her heart aching for what may be upsetting the girl. But after what seemed like a lifetime, Minnie Leigh came back into the café. She'd changed into her work dress, and was tying her apron around her waist.

"Minnie, you don't have to work today. Rest, I'll let you

work when it gets busy, and on Saturday when the weekenders come through. I only have two cabins let out right now, so there won't be many come through here today."

"Now Miss Betty, you know I like to pay my way. I can't let you show me no favorites when Lilly Mae back there working hard as she can go every day. Ain't I one of your workers?"

"Well, um, yes, you do work for me, Minnie," Betty blinked in surprise. "But I don't expect you to work every day while school's in. I know you must be hungry. All you had with you was one little cold sandwich. Lilly Mae has a plate of food all fixed up. Why don't we sit over here you eat? I'll drink a glass of sweet tea, and you can tell me about your first day?"

"Not much to tell, just learn my way today," Minnie shrugged like it was too obvious. Then she remembered something. "Met some new neighbor children and one creepy man. Rest of it was like nothin' I ever knew existed."

"What creepy man?" Betty's eyebrows knitted. "There shouldn't be no man hangin' around the schoolhouse."

"He wasn't there. He came bellowin' in his vehicle right up to the steps where I was a sittin' this morning, letting that old boy Jake out along with his creepy brother."

"Minnie, why do you keep calling them creepy? Did something happen this morning?" the woman asked slowly.

"No, ma'am. That their old man just kept lookin' at me without blinkin', just like that first husband of mine did. Don't like it."

Betty sighed a bit, her face full of concern. "Minnie, you keep saying your *husbands*. Were you really married?"

Minnie Leigh looked up from her plate and, staring with puzzlement over the question, wondered why Miss Betty was asking that question. She already told her several times she was married twice.

"Yes," Minnie nodded. Then she just started talking. "First my dad gave me to this old man. He started out pushin' me through the woods up and over toward his old cabin. Beat me a 'fore we got halfway there. Once we were there, I just did what he told me. Even then he threw me around, drug me by my hair 'til it was comin' out at the roots. After a while, he got tired of me, and traded me off for a mule, cow, and five jugs of shine.

"Now that second husband, I thought he goin' to treat me right. But just four days into it, he comes in after drinkin' shine all night, tryin' to crawl all over me, and I fought and scratch 'til I'd throwed him to the floor. That's when I took off like a light and ran till my chest burnt bad, and next thing you know, I done walked out those woods and down this here road. The good Lawd done brought me right to you'ins door. That it, that's all."

Betty just sat there with her mouth wide open, looking at this beautiful young lady. *How on this green earth did she live through all of this?* Betty gathered herself quickly before Minnie could look up and see the shock on her face.

"I'll be right back, Minnie. Finish your plate." Betty got up, and sprinted for the back door as fast as she could without drawing attention. She barely made it out the door before bursting into tears over what she had just heard.

"How on earth could a child go through all that and still have the heart she does? Lord help me, I love this child even more. How will I ever let her out on her own? Lord help me."

The sky was getting dark. Betty kept calling to the Lord for help, help to guide this young human, how to teach her. Just in a short few minutes, Minnie Leigh had taught her more about broken love, grief, acceptance of what life brings us, and most of all forgiveness, forgiveness of loss that we have no control over. The death of her husband had been devastating, and Betty wasn't sure after all these years if she could honestly say she was over it. Now, she stood here feeling guilty for holding on to the wrong done to her: young bride yet to start a family, which her husband ripped from her before they had a chance to get started.

However, there sat this young child, thrown away by her father to one man that abused her, and from the sounds of it, tried to kill her. Then he shoved her off on another man for mere livestock and liquor. She sat there without any anger in her voice, excited about living today, about her future.

"God, please forgive me for all these wasted years, years of crying and hurting. Thank you for sending this precious young lady into my life."

Betty returned to the table to find Minnie had already removed her plate and replaced it with a slice of pie for both of them. She had placed a cup of coffee out for Betty, fixed just the way the woman liked it. As Betty took her seat at the table, Minnie looked up at her with a content smile on her face. Betty knew at that moment this young lady was her family.

CHAPTER 13

Minnie spent her spare moments between customers and chores, reading through the books given to her by Miss Maple. Betty helped her practice her arithmetic, and would check her handwriting as she learned to form each letter.

Minnie Leigh was surpassing all expectations. She was like a sponge to water, absorbing on contact everything Miss Maple could throw her way. Minnie quickly found that reading was one of her favorite things. By reading, she could do anything. In one book, there was a brother and a sister and their dog that played together, and got into trouble together. It made Minnie wonder why her and her brothers never did anything together. The one she was reading now was about two boys named Tom and Huck. She liked them a lot, since they were always getting into something and going on adventures. She was still a little slow at reading, but she loved it still.

The school term was still young, only in its fifth week, but it seemed to be speeding by. Christmas break would be there before you could wink an eye. Minnie had started leaving a little later, so she could meet up with Sadie and Scotty at the end of their road. Now and again, she would have to wait on them. On those days, she was careful to hide in the shrub at the edge of the road. She was still frightened that Jake's father would pass by and see her when she was alone.

No matter how she tried, she could not shake the creepy feeling he gave her. She was careful to always arrive at school with her friends at her side.

"Minnie, girl, close that book," Betty chuckled. "You need

to get on to school. Remember, Sadie and Scotty are down with influenza. They're not faring well, so don't stop. Sort of a good thing you don't have to wait for them this morning, I'm afraid you might run late. Run along now. Study hard today."

"Lawd mercy, Miss Betty," she quickly packed up. "I movin' fast as my legs will let me." Minnie went out the door with a flash. She was walking so fast she started breaking a sweat.

She slowed her stride as she turned onto the schoolhouse road. But as she approached the schoolhouse, she noticed the door was closed, and there was no one around. All was still and quiet. It was then she saw the paper tacked to the door. Taking her hand, she smoothed the paper out flat. Written on it: "*SCHOOL CLOSED UNTIL FURTHER NOTICE.*"

"After all that runnin' and sweatin'!" Minnie sat down on the steps to catch her breath. She walked to the well and drew up a bucket of cold, clear water, and laughed to herself. "Here I am bein' educated to become a city gal, and I drawin' water from a well again. *Ha!.*" Smiling, she just shook her head as she replaced the ladle. Picking up her books, she headed home.

As she passed Sadie's road, she was so deep in thought that she did not hear the car as it approached. As it passed, it almost hit her, then it pulled off the road in front of her in a spray of dust.

Her knees went weak as soon as she saw him open the door.

As quick as she could, she took off running toward home. But her effort was cut short as he bolted around the front of his car. Grabbing her arm, he threw her against the car. She could already smell the liquor on him.

"Now, where're you runnin' to, gal? All I want to do is talk. Why you'in been avoiding me? I don't see you at the school in the morning no more, and when I come into that fancy café of Betty's, you always disappearing," he slurred, holding her tight.

"Avoidin' you'ins? No need of that, I have nothin' to say to you, old man. Now leave me alone!" Swinging her right hand as hard as she could, she slapped him in the face. She knew it hurt because it whelped up red soon as she hit him.

He didn't release her, and forced Minnie into the back seat of his car. He tightened his grip and caught her right hand stretching both arms above her head.

Minnie became enraged and terrified at the same time. Eyes wild, mind spinning as fast as it could, she tried to figure out how to get away from him. She let out a scream that should've been heard for miles, but when she did, he clasped his free hand over her mouth.

"Why you want to go making all that noise, girl? I don't understand why you're acting this way. I did hear you already been married. It ain't like you no innocent gal. You're *used*, and no one will ever have you. Settle down, just let it happen, you know you want it," he grinned.

Minnie's eyes were wide and scared. As he looked down to pull her dress to her waist, she swung her head back and waited for him to look up. When he did, she threw her forehead into his left eye as hard she could.

For just a moment, he released her as he grabbed his eye. Minnie sprinted from under him, pushing him to the side as she leaped through the door. Just as she was getting her footing, he reached, grabbing her again. All he managed to do was rip her dress almost entirely off her.

She continued running, finally bursting through the café door.

Minnie came in the door, and fell to her knees sobbing. Everyone in the café was frozen seeing their precious friend was beaten and bloody. No one had to ask what had happened. The group of men sitting at their regular table, neighbors, church friends, jumped to their feet.

Lilly Mae's man was coming through the back door with a crate of tomatoes. He slowly placed the crate down, and went to where Minnie knelt on the floor. "Miss Minnie, give big Joe your hand."

"I can't Joe; I can't touch you," she sobbed. Betty stood

frozen in the same spot, seeing her precious girl beaten, her dress torn almost entirely off.

"Now Miss Minnie, you gonna have to trust Big Joe so's we can help you. Who done it, child? Who did this to Big Joe's girl?"

"It was *him*."

"Who, darling?" Lilly Mae asked softly, coming to crouch next to them..

"Jake, Jake Senior."

"Where he now, girl?" Big Joe asked.

"Don't know. He was near Sadie's road." As Minnie fell over onto her back, the last thing she remembered was all the menfolk running through the door yelling at each other.

When Minnie passed out, Big Joe immediately picked her up, and it was then Betty moved to the doors, turning the sign to "*CLOSED,*" and pulling the shades. Betty began to shout orders.

"Lilly Mae, you go fetch the doctor. Hurry, quick as you can! Just turn the stove and oven off. Hurry now! Big Joe, help me get Minnie to her room."

"Yes, ma'am," he followed the woman as Lilly Mae ran out the door.

When the doctor arrived, he examined her and took over cleaning and treating her wounds.

"Well, Doc, did he...did he—?" Betty gasped as she started to cry.

"No," the Doctor shook his head. "No, she must've gotten away from him before he could hurt her anymore."

Betty broke down. "Why? Why this precious child? She already been through enough in her short life. It's just not right."

"Beg your pardon, Miss Betty," the doctor said softly, "but no one deserves this, especially not a female."

"Is she going to be okay? Her breathing isn't right."

"I'm going to sit with her for a bit. She's in shock. It'll be touch and go for a while. I hope she has the strength to pull through," he said, his voice turning concerned. "I'm not going to lie to you, Betty, trauma like this can kill someone. I hate to ask, but I could use some coffee. It's going to be a long day and night,

I'm afraid. I'll not leave her side. And would you mind sending Joe in? I need him to run a couple of errands for me."

"Sure, Doc. Whatever you need me to do, just take care of my girl," Betty nodded through tears.

Soon after, there was a light knock at the door. Doc left the bedside long enough to open the door and let Joe in.

"How is our girl, Doc?"

"Not good, Joe. If she doesn't fight or have the strength to fight, she'll die."

The statement rocked Big Joe to the core. His emotions went from anger, wishing he could have gone with the other men to give Jake Sr. his up and comings. But as quick as that emotion ran through him, he was overcome with grief and concern for the young girl that had managed to get into everyone's heart. Joe felt his faith falter for a moment.

"Joe, I need you to run some errands for me. Could you do that? I don't want to leave her," the Doctor explained.

"Sure, Doc. Whatever I can do to help, you know that."

"Okay. First, go straight over to the preacher's house. Let him know what's happing over here. Tell him to come quick. Then, you go to my house and fetch my wife. I need her help. Betty's not going to be in any shape to help. Then gather this list of supplies," he handed a list to Joe, "and bring it back as quick as lighting. Go now. Hurry, Joe."

Joe left without saying a word, walking fast, almost running but not. He did not want anyone to panic, especially Betty. Minnie Leigh might need her.

Betty came back into the room with coffee and a slice of pie.

"How is she by now, Doc?"

"No change yet, Betty. But I can't let you sit with her yet. I need to be here just in case things go bad. I sent for my wife. What I want *you* to do is go bake some cakes or pies, stay busy."

"I won't have any problem with that. The café is filling up with folks that have already heard what happened," Betty remarked. "They're all here to pray and be here when she wakes up. I'll be busy feeding them."

"Seems backward, I know," Doc said. "But it's the best thing you can do, stay busy. Now, don't wear yourself to a frazzle. You sit when you need to. And you can come and check on her from time to time."

"I understand, Doc." Betty bent down, kissing her girl on the forehead ever so lightly. There was a significant black, indented area to the right side of her forehead where Minnie had used it as a weapon.

After what seemed like an eternity, Joe and Doc's wife arrived.

"Good you're here. Her respirations are slower, and she's cold and clammy. Joe, find me some blankets. Just bring a pile of them, we need to warm her." Looking at his wife, he said, "I need the cuff and meter. I need to see where her pressure is. I'm going to need your help here most of the night. Is your mom with the kids?"

"Yes, she is. When she heard about Minnie, she decided to stay home knowing you might need me."

"Good, good, because it looks like it's going to be all night, and if she doesn't pull through, I'll need your help with Betty."

The café was busier than it had been in a very long time. There was a hush over the crowd, not the typical loud laughter and banter. All were there to support Minnie, help her pull through.

As Betty went from table to table, everyone assured her of their prayers for her girl. Betty appreciated all the support, and the distraction was keeping her mind occupied. However, every time someone came through the back door, she jumped. Eventually someone must have noticed though, because the next time she looked in that direction, there was a sizeable handwritten notice that read: *"USE FRONT DOOR AND WALK AROUND THE BUILDING. MINNIE NEEDS YOU TO BE QUIET!!!"*

Betty laughed at the note. It was straightforward, and to the point. Anyone could have written it. Directness is the East Tennessee way. No one here ever saw the sense in beating around the bush about anything. Might be why people have survived these mountains for so long.

A truck with about six men in it came barreling into the parking lot and around to the back. They looked rough, and Betty ran to the door to keep them quiet. As she approached the truck, she saw a man's feet hanging over the back. When she looked up, the group was watching her. Her face must have shown her fear.

"He's not dead, Miss Betty. Not that he doesn't deserve it. He's just out cold. We need to ask Doc a question though. One of the boys thinks he has done gone and broke one of Jake Senior's arm and a leg." They all tried not to smile at this, knowing Miss Betty didn't approve of vengeance.

"You stay right here and keep quiet." Betty stepped to the door and spoke in whispers to the Doctor.

As he approached the truck, he said, "Howdy boys."

"Howdy Doc," they answered.

"What do we have here? Now, how you know he ain't dead?" Doc asked.

"He still breathing, ain't he?"

"Looks like it," Doc said. "Boys, I don't have time for this, that child in there might not make it. Just do what you would do if you in the woods and broke yourself up. Then take him to the jail. Turn him over to the sheriff. Let him wake up locked in a cage where he belongs."

"Okay, Doc. We just wanted to check with you."

As Doc glanced at the unconscious man again, he chuckled as he examined the left eye socket.

"Our girl's pretty tough, isn't she? He'll probably lose that left eye where she hit him with her forehead. It's clotted up pretty bad."

"It was like that when we finally found him, before we ever touch him," the men explained.

"I'm sure it was. Minnie Leigh's forehead looks just as bad. She's not faring as well as he is, though. Pray boys, pray is all I can say," Doc reminded them.

At this, the men hung their heads. The driver slowly and quietly began to back the truck, turning the wheels, then pulled slowly around the building and onto the highway to take their catch to the jailhouse.

While Betty was outside, the preacher arrived. After going in praying over Minnie, he returned to the café where he joined the crowd, offering handshakes and questions for the ones he had not seen in church lately. All had 'good' reasons for not attending, and just as he was trained to do, he had a quick reply rebutting their reasonings for not participating.

Betty came in and took a seat at the counter, quietly watching as her community gathered to bring Minnie back by sheer presence and will.

It was now late evening, and there was no change. But even though they were in a café, some of the ladies brought in food to help feed the crowd. Ladies buzzed back and forth from the kitchen to the dining area, hauling in full plates of food, and gathering and washing the used ones. Some of the youngest children began to whine from being confined indoors. The young mothers didn't want to leave. However, they gathered their little ones and kissed their husbands, leaving them to bring the news home, good or bad.

Hugs were given out freely to neighbors all around. Though these neighbors did not always agree, they did stand up for each other when one of them became a victim of life, weather, accident, illness, or crime. They stood beside each other and gave strength. Minnie had quickly become a member of this community. With her quick wit, smile, and hard work, she was an example to all of them. Here and there, you could hear stories of her escape from the mountain, how she had made her way there to Bean Station.

As the sun disappeared below the horizon, the Doctor came through the back door. Everyone stopped and held their breath.

"No change," he shook his head, "just need to stretch my

legs and refill my coffee cup."

There was a collected exhale as everyone breathed easier knowing she was still fighting for her life. Betty escaped to her cabin for a while. There she could let her tears flow and fall to her knees to pray.

"Lord, with all that I am, I want to ask your forgiveness for not protecting this gift you brought into my life," yet as soon as she pleaded and cried, there came a calm. In the calm, there was an assurance that this tragic event was in no way her fault.

"Father, how wonderful you are. The Bible says in our grief, we will be comforted. I wish I'd realized sooner that was all I had to do. When Andrew was killed, all I could do was to be angry with you, and wonder why you would bring such pain into my life. Now I realize it's not you that brings the suffering, but the one that is bent on destroying it. I ask that you heal Minnie, allow her to grow old and be blessed with all that is good. If Knoxville is where you want her, I'll not try to talk her out of it any longer. She's yours."

Betty gathered herself up went and put on a fresh shirt and returned to the café. As she approached the back door, she stopped briefly at the table that held the face bowl and washed her face. Big Joe walked up behind her.

"Any change?"

Betty turned with a start.

"Sorry, ma'am I didn't mean to scare you," he apologized.

"It's ok, Joe. I'm a little jumpy. To answer your question, I was just fixing to stick my head in and check on her. Come along with me, we'll go together."

Betty knocked lightly on the door and opened it. The doctor was removing some of the bed covering.

"Good, glad you're here. I think Minnie might be coming out of it," the Doctor smiled. "She began to warm up just a short while ago. Her color is starting to return. Would you let the others know? She's not out of the woods yet, but hopefully, she'll continue to come around. We should know in a couple more hours."

"I will."

Betty and Joe quietly left the room, letting the Doctor continue to tend to Minnie.

Betty went into the café, and let everyone know about Minnie Leigh's improvements. Everyone was grateful for the news, yet no one left. Betty stepped to the kitchen door and told Lilly Mae that she could go, but Lilly stood her ground. "No ma'am, I'm just fine right here."

"Okay, if that's what you want to do. Thank you, Lilly, thank you for all you do."

Three hours passed. Doc's wife came running through the door.

"Betty! Betty, come quick!"

Everyone that was sitting stood up once again. They held their breath as they watched Betty run out of the back door, drained of all her color.

As she flew into the room, Doc moved away from the bed.

"Hey. Miss Betty. Sorry I scared you so," Minnie spoke in a soft, weak voice.

Betty's tears flowed from happiness. "It's okay dear," she whispered. She planted a soft kiss on Minnie's cheek.

"I think I'll rest a little while longer before I get up, if that okay."

"Sure, sure! Rest my dear, rest as long as you want to."

After Minnie was sleeping soundly, everyone left the room, knowing that she was going to make a full recovery.

The cheers and rebel calls were enough to wake the dead. Minnie woke for just a brief moment. Smiling to herself, she drifted off into a peaceful rest.

Just two days later, the sheriff came in for a morning cup of coffee. As Minnie turned around to fetch his coffee, the sheriff turned on his stool.

"Say Betty, did you hear about Jake Senior? He had himself a bad vehicle accident. When I got there, he was out cold, all broke up, and that's not all. The bed of his truck was full of shine. I do hate it, but he off to the Big House for a while," the Sheriff raised his eyebrows knowingly.

Betty gave a slight nod to the sheriff. Nothing else was ever said about Jake Sr, and just a couple of days later, the students at the schoolhouse were informed that Jake Jr, his brother, and mother, had to move to Arkansas to take care of their ailing grandmother.

CHAPTER 14

"Will she ever get here?" Minnie, Betty, and Sadie were waiting on Miss Maple to arrive with the results of Minnie's final exams.

"Settle down, child," Lilly Mae said. "Don't rush your life. It passes fast enough on its own."

"I know, Lilly. It's like Christmas Eve when you just can't wait for Christmas morning to arrive, so that you can tear into all the presents. The anticipation, the dread, and the joy."

"Woohoo, listen to our girl with her fancy words! *An-ti-ci-pa-tion*," Sadie said, separating each syllable with a smile.

Betty was sitting on her stool at the counter figuring the books, smiling to herself to be witness to the transformation in Minnie. In a little less than a year, the rough, uneducated girl had disappeared, replaced with a beautiful, educated young lady.

What was the most amazing thing to witness was how Minnie Leigh transformed, but maintained her mountain spirit. She hadn't lost who she was at the core. The young girl that rose early to *greet the day*, eyes filled with the wonder of the valley below her mountain, Ginseng digging, hunting, fishing, barefoot ragtag—the heartbroken girl was still there. Minnie was like a vase broken but glued back together. It remained the same vase. Though crushed and cracked, the damage was not apparent.

"Oh my, there she is! Here she comes!" Minnie almost screamed with excitement.

The screen door of the café opened. Miss Maple, with her slow gliding steps, entered the room with a beaming smile, papers in hand.

"Well?" Sadie was as anxious as her friend. This moment was hope and closure to all the pain, and a new door opening.

Miss Maple found a neutral space in the room so that all present would hear the announcement.

"It is with a full heart, and my deepest pleasure, to announce that Minnie Leigh Robertson has graduated from Bean Station School House with the highest marks ever awarded. Minnie, it is with pride that I give you your diploma."

Minnie stepped forward and took the parchment in her hand, not believing her eyes though she could feel the physical object in her hand. She could not quite believe what she had accomplished.

Betty was the first to congratulate her with a hug. But she lingered, knowing that soon, Minnie would want to realize her dream of working and living on her own in Knoxville

Standing next to her friend Sadie, Minnie grabbed the other girl, jumped up and down, and spun them together in celebration. In a rare moment, Lilly Mae left the kitchen, and joined in the celebration and to hug her young co-worker and friend. She shed tears, thinking of the life she'd been privileged to share. Big Joe entered the café as the ladies calmed. With a shuffle step and a short Flat-Foot dance, he advanced toward Minnie, picking her high up off the ground to spin her around once and set her back on her feet. "You're a real blessin' to know, Miss Minnie, a real blessin' indeed. Your Big Joe is proud of you, gal, yes sir, real proud."

"You know what we need, Miss Betty?"

"What's that, Sadie?"

"We need to have one of those real mountain hoedowns. Music, food, and friends. This is a really special moment for Minnie, don't you think?" she smiled wide.

"Well Minnie Leigh, what do you think about that? Would you like to have a *hoedown*?" Betty chuckled.

"Would I! I've not been to one since I was a real young girl. Everyone is laughing and dancing. Just a perfect time."

"Then we'll plan it and get the word out to everyone."

As things started to settle back into the usual routine of the café, Minnie excused herself.

"I'll be back shortly. I want to put my diploma up so nothin' happens to it."

"Okay dear, take your time."

Entering her room, Minnie shut the door, leaning her back against it. She closed her eyes, and let out a squeal. After putting her diploma away, she left her room, but instead of returning to the café, Minnie took a path she herself had created that led to the back of Betty's property. There was an open field that rolled gently down and back up, twenty acres of open area. It had become the place where she greeted the day, or just escaped to to talk to God, read, or just flee to solitude.

"God, are you there? It's Minnie Leigh. If you are, I just want to thank you. Thank you for givin' me dreams fulfilled, dreams I never knew I had. I come down that mountain to find a safe place is all. And what did you go and do? You did give me a home, a new family, friends, and now you allowed me to be educated. Did you see my diploma? I should have brought it and showed it to you.

"God, I been thinkin' that it might not be you that caused my Paw and Tolbert to trade me, but if'n they had not, I would not have anything I have. I don't know how you done it, but you did it. You did give me more than I could ever hold.

"Well, I better get back before everyone gets in a panic. Just wanted you to know I appreciate my diploma."

Minnie was light footed as she walked back to the café.

"Where've you been?" Sadie asked with a big smile. "I have everything worked out. We're going to use Miss Betty's field. We'll have everyone that has a vehicle pull them up in a big circle, and build the biggest bonfire you ever saw. Paw knows some mountain folk that plays really well. They play in Knoxville now and again. Everyone can bring a dish. There'll be plenty to eat. We'll laugh, dance, and tell stories! It'll be plum fun."

"Sounds nice. I have one question though, what mountain

do those singers come from? I don't want no one runnin' tel-lin' my Paw, or worse, one of my husbands, where I am," Minnie laughed a bit.

"Oh, Minnie I didn't even think of that. I'll try and find out."

"Okay. If you can make sure they're not from my mountain, I'll be okay with that."

"You girls are going to have to spread the word for about a week to make sure everyone knows," Betty stated.

"We'll handle all of that, Miss Betty. Minnie and I will take my horse every day and spread the word. In a few days, the whole valley will be here."

The girls spent their free mornings spreading the word. Some of the menfolk started gathering wood for the bonfire. Another group even built a wooden floor on a low frame for dancing and flat-footing.

But for the second time in a week, melancholy overcame Minnie. She felt she was saying goodbye.

"Lilly, Miss Lilly!"

"Yes, child, what wrong? Is my girl okay?"

"I don't know Lilly. I think I'm dying."

"Why do you say that, girl?" Lilly Mae's eyes widened. "You feel ok? Do I need to fetch Doc?"

"No! Don't. Just wait," Minnie shook her head.

"Minnie girl, what goin' on? Tell Lilly."

"I just keep getting this feelin' that I sayin' goodbye to everything around here. Am I dying?"

"Lord child, we all get way once in a while."

"No, this is deep, Lilly, like I can reach out and grab it. When I was studying for my exams, I kept feeling it was the end of everything I have come to know." Suddenly overwhelmed, Minnie teared up.

Lilly Mae reached out and hugged her tight. "You just hang on to Lilly, child. Hang on tight, I won't let you go, you hear."

Shaking her head and hanging on to her friend, Minnie knew it would still not be enough. Even now she felt herself, and saw herself, turn, waving with a smile as she walked out the door.

CHAPTER 15

The day of the party arrived with much to do. The café was closed. Tables and chairs had been moved out to the field on Betty's insistence. The temporary long table had been built to hold the food. People started gathering early. Those that had to travel some distance had shown up the night before and camped. Everyone was clean; new overalls for the men, new dresses or ribbons for the girls.

"You would think we had a new preacher coming for a tent meeting the way everyone all spit and shinin'."

"They jus' loves our girl; she somethin' special."

Big Joe and Lilly Mae were sitting on the tailgate of his truck watching all the preparation. Once in a while, the men would stop and speak to Joe, laughing and joking. The ladies would bow their heads in greeting and stand to the side while the men chatted back and forth.

Lilly Mae did not address the other women, which had always made her feel like she was rude. When she and Joe came to work for Miss Betty, she learned quickly that east Tennessee valley folk had a different manner of communicating. Certain things were just not tolerated. Like now, if menfolk were any-where around, women were expected to stay quiet. Bar the ini-tial greeting. She had always chosen to let go of what seemed right to her, and except the customs of the people she would be living around.

The crowd began to grow, and the bonfire was started, though it was still light out. The musicians were setting up their chairs and adjusting and tuning their instruments.

"Lilly, should we go up to Miss Betty's cabin and offer to drive her down?"

"That would probably be welcomed. Miss Betty is always on her feet."

When they arrived, Sadie was standing at the door knocking. Instead of getting out of his truck, he yelled out of the window.

"Ask Miss Betty if she'd like a ride out to the field."

"Sure thing, Joe," Sadie answered.

The door swung open. Standing in the doorway was Minnie Leigh in a mint-colored dress, a simple A-line not as full in the skirt as most girls liked. But the contrast of the green and Minnie's strawberry blonde hair made quite a statement.

"Woo-wee! None of the fellows will look at anyone but you tonight!"

"Quit joshin' me, Sadie. Betty insisted I have a new dress for the party. I didn't know she even bought it until this morning. Last week, she was gone when I got up, and Lilly and I ran the café by ourselves all day. You know where she had gone off to?"

"No. Where?"

"She went clear to Knoxville to buy it," Minnie sighed a bit. "She could've taken me with her. Miss Betty knows how much I've always wanted to see Knoxville. When I asked her why, she just said she had seen my time to leave and it's not today. Now, what kind of answer was that?"

"I don't know," Sadie shrugged. "Sometimes though, it seems like she can see the future. Like she a witch or something."

They did not see when Betty entered the room.

"A witch, am I?" Betty suddenly said. "Well Sadie, if you spread that tale to the wrong person, ya'll will be standin' at my bonfire. Only, I'll be the one on the stake in the middle of the fire."

"Don't say things like that, Miss Betty."

"Well, how do you think all those innocent women got burnt at the stake? It's not just up north, you know," she explained. "Back home there are healers, seers, mountain witches, and they were all real, and all had their magic. No one would dare burn or hang one of them. I know how to make potion's and medicine with herbs, but I'm not a witch.

"There's an *herb man* in Knoxville. He sells roots and leaves with healing powers, and that doesn't make him a witch. But enough of this talk," she shook her head. "Everyone started to arrive, and we must be there to greet our guests."

Betty shooed them out of the house and closed the door. Joe was still waiting, and Minnie and Sadie climbed up into the bed of the truck. Betty had slid into the front seat next to Lilly Mae.

As they drove up, they could hear music as it played. There was no dancing yet, just toe tapping and hand clapping. The crowd was waiting for the guest of honor. As Betty and Minnie walked through the crowd and crossed the open space to the temporary dance floor, the music went quiet, and a hush fell over the crowd.

Betty addressed the crowd first. "Shy a year ago, as I walked out of the café one morning, I saw what appeared a young boy collapse at the edge of the highway. When I knelt beside the fallen, I could see that the person before me was a young girl," she paused. "Minnie was exhausted and hungry. She'd made her way from *her* mountain to our valley. And from the day she fell into my life, she has taught me.

"I didn't realize it at the time, but I'd closed myself off to loving anyone outside of my misery. But with her melodic mountain speech, profound but simple knowledge of life, and mountain straightforwardness, she's become my family and changed me forever.

"She's matured and grown. She's made her way into everyone's heart. She's never asked for anything, but has given freely." Looking Minnie Leigh in the eyes, she said, "Minnie, you have become a part of our little community, you are family. Now you have gone and made us proud by graduating with the highest marks ever made by a local! Now, we want to give back in a small way to you, with this party. If you stay here and build a life or travel on, you'll always be one of us."

Minnie received a wave of claps, whistling, and rebel yells. She sniffed some tears away.

"I don't know what to say. It's been every one of you'ins that have given to me. I thank you! Now, where's that music?" Suddenly kicking her shoes off her feet, she began flat foot dancing. With the lightness of a child in her heart, she danced, and the band of musicians watched and followed her lead, joining in with the familiar mountain music. Others joined her, and soon the crowd was laughing and dancing. The smell of food as the dishes was uncovered, mingled with the scent of the wood burning, brought out a festive mood.

Minnie continued walking around with bare feet, enjoying the feel of the grass as it cooled and damped beneath her feet. Her heart was light with the love that surrounded her, and heaviness that she'd be leaving soon.

At some point, she spotted a crowd that had formed behind a group of trucks. Walking over, Minnie smiled and shook her head at the familiar sight of the passing of the jug. "What you'ins doin', fellers?"

"Now, Minnie, you need to go and let us fellers get about our business."

"It's my party, so that you can put that man folk talk up somewhere."

As Minnie held their attention, the Sheriff walked up behind them.

"Boys." With not another word, the Sheriff reached out to receive the jug as it was surrendered to the lawman.

"Now you fellers know liquor is illegal. We have us the *law of prohibition*," he said slowly.

Minnie was standing there holding her breath, not knowing what to do. To her, having a jug of shine at a hoe down was as natural as having a pitcher of sweet tea to any southerner. Then the Sheriff laid the jug upon his shoulder, pulled the cork took a big draw of the liquid. Smacking his lips, as he lowered the jug and recorked it.

"Glad you knew better than to bring illegal liquor to Minnie's celebration." Handing the jug to Minnie as he passed, he patted her on the head and gave her shoulder a squeeze, whispering, "I think the ladies have a jug of their own over near the food spread." He just shuffled off with a little flat foot move and a smile.

"Lawd," one of the fellers said, "ny gizzard done flipped around in my chest!"

Minnie tipped her head. "Have a good time, feller."

Walking away, she headed for the food spread. She was getting a little hungry, and she longed to have a small nip of shine. Minnie did not drink, but a sip now and then even as a young child made her feel like she was a part of something no one else was. After fixin' herself a plate, Minnie weaved around the cars, but did not see a gathering of women that might be sippin'.

"You're looking for something?" Minnie heard the familiar voice of Sadie as she approached.

"Well, I...I was um, just lookin'..."

"Are you looking for the ladies and the shine?" Sadie raised an eyebrow.

"Well, yes."

"Betty ran them loose gals into the woods."

"Why? It's a party." Minnie was confused.

"Yes, I's going to stay a party until the end. But we're not going to have a bunch of drunk women folk fightin'."

"Now why would Betty think, just causes their havin' a nip they going to end up in a fist-fight?" Minnie chuckled.

"Women folk got too much emotion to drink hooch," Sadie said matter-of-factly.

"Well I've been drinkin' shine since before I can remember."

"I'm sure you have, Minnie," Sadie said, her face blank. "But you're not living on the mountain anymore. It's important what others think. The Good Book says to be an example of all that's good."

"Well, I ain't read that book yet," Minnie shrugged.

"Still the same," Sadie frowned. "It's important, especially if you go leaving us to live on your own somewhere else." She paused, and then suddenly started to cry. "Why're you leaving us still? *Why*, Minnie? Why after all we've done been through together?" Then Sadie turned and left, leaving Minnie standing by herself.

The pulling away from her had already begun. It was unspoken. No one, especially those closest to her, wanted to confront their loss.

The party began to fade as one family, then another, said their goodbyes. The only ones remaining were those that would pack up and leave out early in the morning before the sun. Minnie spoke to as many as she could, and enjoyed a few last dances with one and then the other. She continued to carry the sadness of parting, but was excited too.

The days following the party were slow and quiet. The locals that frequented the café were still friendly as always, but an unspoken pulling away had set in. Word had gotten around that Minnie was leaving. No one, not even Minnie, knew when.

One morning not a week later, Minnie entered the café as she usually did. She was not dressed for work. She'd donned her new dress, and was wearing her overcoat. As Minnie set her suitcase down, Betty said nothing. She was watching the suitcase, willing it not to be there.

"Would you give me a ride over to the train depot this morning?" Minnie asked.

"Are you sure this is what you want?" Betty asked softly.

"Miss Betty, I know you don't want me to leave, but if I don't go and live on my own, I'll always have a trapped feeling inside. Now that the day is here, I find myself pulled to stay. I must go just to see what's there. Who knows? I may be back like a scalded cat. Bean Station is the most significant town I've ever been to. I'm just curious what rest of the world holds."

"Curiosity killed the cat!" Lilly Mae put in from her place in the kitchen.

"Idleness is the devil's playground," Minnie answered, smiling.

And just like that, Minnie said her goodbyes to all present, and went to the car and waited for Betty.

CHAPTER 16

As the Landlord stood at the door to one of the small rooms she let, she rattled off what the weekly rent covered.

Minnie Leigh was disappointed at what she saw. In her imagination, she pictured a small, clean room with pretty drapery on the windows. But the places Minnie had looked at today were all dirty, dingy, and gray. Not one of them had drapes on the windows.

No matter. she would have to decide on one or the other for now.

When she boarded the train near Tate Springs early that morning, she'd imagined that she'd exit the train in Knoxville, and find a town as she had formed in her mind. The pictures in her mind had come from reading books and looking at the illustrations found in them. Minnie had no personal example of a town or city.

Mountain homes were scattered here and there throughout the mountainside. There was a mercantile on the mountain road, but no other store or business of any kind. You could buy or order anything you wanted or needed, and you could also receive or post your mail.

Drawn back from her thoughts by the Landlady asking: "Do you want it or not, gal?" Minnie rolled her eyes, but agreed to the terms. She was tired of carrying her new suitcase full of her belongings from place to place. She would plan to eat the small pack of food Lilly Mae had sent with her tonight, and tomorrow find a job. She'd saved enough money to last her for a few weeks. But now, she thought it might run out sooner than she planned.

She sat alone now on the edge of the bed. "While it's still daylighted out, I could get out and possibly find work." She paused then, and sighed. "Oh my, there I go talking to myself again. If anyone hears me, they'll think I'm touched."

Minnie pushed her suitcase under the bed, and locked the door as she left. Getting directions and information from the Landlord—who was sitting on a stool behind the counter—Minnie struck out on the streets of Knoxville.

The landlord had informed her that jobs were starting to fall off due to the political unrest surrounding the City Manager. A new City Manager had been hired again to straighten out the finical problems that plagued Knoxville. He was often heard to say that the more he looked and dug into the issues of Knoxville, the more issues he found.

It was suggested that Minnie Leigh ask for work at The Golden Sun Café near the Market House.

There were new streetcars that provided transportation; however, Minnie preferred to walk. She quickly found that walking in woman's high heels was probably the reason most chose to utilize the streetcar service.

Arriving at the café, she found a very fast-paced establishment. Walking through the café doors, she was overwhelmed by the sheer size of the dining area. She had become accustomed to the small, quaint dining at Miss Betty's. As one server after another passed by her, she tried without success to find out who she should speak to so to inquire about employment. Taking a seat at the first open chair she could find, she was soon approached by a young lady asking for her order.

"I don't want to place an order at this time, I'd like to know whom to speak to about a job?"

"If you're not eating, you need to move for a paying customer," the server quipped.

"Be glad to, just point out where I can find the owner," Minnie huffed.

"Just over there at the end of the counter."

Sliding out of the chair, freeing it for a *paying customer*, Minnie stood, straightened her dress, and walked up to a gentleman not much taller than herself. He had a round face, big eyes, thick, full white mustache on his upper lip, and he had a full, round belly that moved when he looked up to speak. His apron was stretched so tight that the apron strings looked as if they would break at any moment.

As she approached the man, he was speaking, which to Minnie sounded like made-up words with an accent she had never heard before.

Sticking out her hand to shake his, she said, "Hello sir, my name's Minnie Leigh Robertson. I'm looking for employment. I have a reference letter from Miss Betty of Bean Station where I lived and was previously employed."

"I'm Kallergis, one of the owners." The gentleman stood there quiet for a moment, surprised, but curious. "Well, where is it?"

"Where's what, sir?" Minnie blinked.

"The letter."

"Oh!" her eyes widened. "Yes sir, here it is." Reaching into her bag, Minnie pulled out the envelope Miss Betty had given her to present whenever she applied for a position.

"Nice, good," the man stated as he looked over the letter. "How is it this Miss Betty would recommend you here?"

"She previously lived in Knoxville. Before her husband was killed, they had often took a meal here. She says the food was good. She also said you never lacked for customers."

"She's right, she's right," he smiled. "Well tell me, if I gave you a job, when could you start?"

"Now. Today," Minnie said, trying to hide her excitement.

With a smile and a nod of the head, the man said, "Unless you have a dress and stockings and proper shoes, you will need today and tomorrow the gather everything. Do you have money to buy them, or do you want it taken out of your pay every day?"

She held her head up and straight. "I have my own money."

"Okay, then you come back in two days. One of the girls

will show you the ropes."

"What time do you open?"

"We never close," explained. "Come early if you want to catch the early crowd. Four or five in the morning would be good. That is when folks come by on their way to work the quarry, mills, and factories."

Minnie shook the little man's hand, turned, and walked out of the café beaming. The gentleman had directed Minnie to the other side of the vast Market House that seemed to sit in the middle of everything on these few blocks. There, she found the mercantile he'd directed her to. She told the clerk what she needed, and the clerk gathered the proper dress from somewhere in the back. Minnie thought that the dress material looked thin, but while inquiring about it, she remembered Miss Betty had taught her that was the reason women wore petty coats under their dresses.

Minnie Leigh forgot all about the streetcars, she was too excited. Her evening was spent in her room, eating the cold food she had in her bag, and reading a fashion magazine sh'd bought while she was at the mercantile. It was her first purchase of something just for enjoyment. As she flipped through the pages, she became embarrassed when she turned the page to see ladies in undergarments right there for everyone to see. She looked back and forth over her shoulder, just as if someone was in the room with her.

The sun had set. Minnie looked through the window and noticed that there were gas lanterns on a tall post that lined the street. The crowd, though much thinner, was still moving around. Music could be heard, and the smell of various foods as they cooked in the nearby restaurants could be smelled. Liquor was illegal in town, she'd found out. It made her question why so many people milled about.

"How can anyone stay up so late eating and shopping when one has to be up very early to work?" If Minnie Leigh had not secured a job the first day, she wondered if she would have gotten straight on the train and headed back to Betty's. Culture shock was already starting to set in.

Minnie dressed for bed. She'd left word at the desk to wake her around three AM. It was not long before she dozed off.

CHAPTER 17

Minnie was up early and dressed in her uniform, stockings, and shoes. She left her room, locking the door behind her.

When Minnie arrived on time at four AM, the Café was already busy. As she entered the door, she was greeted by another gentleman.

"You must be our new girl. I'm Callimachi. You met my cousin yesterday. Okay, might as well just jump in, let's see where to start you."

Leading Minnie to a back room, he pointed out where she could place her bag, and gave her an apron. Callimachi inspected her to make sure her uniform was presentable.

"Okay young lady, just to run you through the way things work around here. We have a *Daily Special*, first to serve one in town. Specials usually consist of lamb. It pleases our Italian and Syrian friends. If anyone orders fish, you let me or one of my cousins in the kitchen know. They will run over to the Market House and choose a fresh fish.

"Hamburgers and fish sandwiches are five cents, bowl of chili ten cents, beef stew fifteen cents. Steak dinner, with three vegetables, dessert, and drink is twenty cents, fifteen cents without meat. If they want T-bone dinner, it is twenty-five cents."

"I'll work on the menu."

"Yea, yea, you will get it soon enough. You have worked café before?"

"Yes, sir, one a lot smaller than this one. In Bean Station."

"Awe yes, Tate Springs Resort is in Bean Station?"

"Yes, close by. You've been there before?" she asked.

"No, the misses always wanting to go. Can't take her, restaurant too busy these days," he shrugged. "Okay, I want you to follow one of the other girls, let her explain things to you, help her out if it gets busy. Catch on fast as you can so you can get your own line of customers. We will set you a section up where you can seat them when they come in for a meal."

As the girl began to explain the way things worked, she was impressed to see that Minnie was very comfortable seating each of her tables and taking an occasional order.

It wasn't long before she began to feel she was already one of the girls.

Her first day was busy, and she often felt she was moving in slow motion. The menu was rarely in need, as most customers were regulars. She quickly found out though, that the owners did indeed send one of the girls or cousins out to buy ingredients to cook things not on the menu. He was very accommodating to the customers, not wanting to lose them to any of the other cafés and restaurants located in the market.

As Minnie approached one table around noon, one of the gentlemen was more interested to find out where she came from and where she lived now. Minnie kept a smile on her face and just repeated: "May I take your order?"

"Now hear, girly, you'll find that we're very friendly folk here in Knoxville. If a gentleman is just trying to be friendly, the polite thing to do is just be friendly back."

"I am friendly, just not any of your business where I live," she shrugged.

"What? You haven't learned who I am? I can help you get settled right in," he said with a sly smile on his face.

"I don't need no man to help me *settle in*. I can do just fine by myself," Minnie narrowed her eyes.

"Woo-*oooh*. Listen to that sass! Headstrong, I like me a headstrong gal. But that sass won't get you anywhere around here."

Minnie sighed. "Sir, I'll give you time to decide what it is you want to eat, then I'll come back and get your order." Minnie turned to walk away, but the gentleman grabbed her arm. Turning quickly around, she looked the man dead in his eyes. "Mister, you let go of me *now*. I don't take kindly to no man grabbing me just when he wants to. Where I come from, you can lose your arm for even thinking about grabbing a lady." Minnie lied. She hoped that she was convincing.

Just as the man went to explain who he was again, Callimachi stepped up. "Now Mr. Gregory, you have been told about grabbing our girls."

"I'm just trying to get to know the new girl," he smiled.

"You go get to know some *other* girl, this is not a brothel."

"No, it sure isn't. But you got some real pretty, friendly girls in here," he chuckled.

"So, give Minnie your order, eat, and leave. Come back when you learn your place in here."

"Yes sir!" he said with a half-hearted salute.

Minnie worked her way through lunch services, then took a short break out behind the café. There she found a co-worker smoking. As Minnie joined her in the alley, the young girl introduced herself as Julia.

"You don't sound like you're from around here," Minnie noted.

"I'm not," said Julia. "I came here with my parents from New York City, New York when I was much younger. My parents were killed last year, so I live on my own. I'm saving to move to Dallas. They say it's a much bigger place than Knoxville, and I hear is a lot cleaner. There are substantial fancy stores, museums, and even a zoo there," she smiled.

"What's a zoo?" Minnie asked.

"*What's a zoo?!* You're not from here either, are you?"

"No, I from the highest mountain peak before you get to Johnson City."

"My goodness girl, how on earth, and *why* on earth did you come to Knoxville?" Julia laughed.

"It's a long story, and we don't have time. We need to get

in there and clean up our tables. I'm sure there's another group of customers waiting by now."

"It stays busy around here. We come in very early and stay until the sun goes down," Minnie's co-worker explained.

"I am not scared to work," Minnie said.

The girls smoothed their dresses and headed back inside. Just like Minnie thought, there were tables with dirty dishes and most importantly her tips. She jumped right in and began to clean. Julia, on the other hand, stopped to talk to one of the other servers.

The day seemed to slow down. Minnie busied herself sweeping the floor and straightening chairs. When she went back into the kitchen, she found that the dirty dishes were piling up, and no one was washing them. She rolled her sleeves up, donned another apron, and began to wash.

"Gal, I wish I had more like you," said the owner. "You know I'm not paying you to wash?"

"Yes, I do, but the dishes were piling up, and we might need them later."

"You're right, we will probably need them. I'm just not used to anyone doing anything except their job." Taking her hands, he said, "Okay, that's enough. I'm going to let you go—"

Minnie turned quickly on her heels. "*Let me go?* What did I do wrong?"

"Nothing," he raised an eyebrow.

"Then why are you letting me go?"

"Oh! No, not firing you," he quickly explained. "I am going to let you go on home. Customers have slowed, and since it is your first day, I figured you might want to go. It has been a hectic morning, and I don't want you so tired you cannot work tomorrow. Just come in early like you did this morning."

"Okay," Minnie let out a breath of relief. "I'm a might tired. Miss Betty's café is nowhere as big as this place."

"I am sure it is not. But Bean Station is nowhere near the size of Knoxville."

Minnie Leigh removed the outer apron. After emptying

her tips into her pocketbook, she removed the apron that was part of her uniform. She folded the apron as small as she could, and placed it in her purse.

Minnie decided to stroll and explore the market. It wasn't long before she noticed there were musicians all over the area, most of them blind. There was a mixture of blues and hillbilly music that could be heard around the market.

Minnie strolled along, looking at the fashions displayed in the various windows. There were street vendors scattered everywhere selling their wares. One could find anything they wanted here, and Minnie bought a hot sandwich. She laughed at herself for doing so, but she was hungry after working around food all day. Even though she was tired, and her feet began to ache, she strolled back to her little room.

When she entered the room, she viewed it differently than she had before. There was just something about working a job she had accrued for herself, and though the room was not anywhere near the finest, it was hers—paid with money she had earned waiting tables at Betty's diner.

Minnie set on the one chair in the room, kicked off her shoes, and unwrapped her sandwich. Before she knew it, the sandwich was gone. Next, she slipped her shoes on, and walked to the desk to ask to be awakened again at three AM. Returning to her room, she poured water into a wash basin, and washed her face, arms, armpits, then sat down and washed her tired feet.

She then readied herself for bed. Climbing under the covers, she noticed that the sun had not quite set. It was the last thing she remembered until she was awakened the next morning to repeat the day before.

One day led to the next, and before long, she realized she had been in Knoxville for two months. She and Sadie had stayed in touch, sending postcards back and forth. Sadie always ended hers with *seeing you soon*. Minnie didn't think that Sadie meant that she would actually see her soon, she just took it as a lovely little salutation.

And from time to time, there was one from Betty, always with good wishes from Lilly Mae and Joe.

CHAPTER 18

One evening two months later, as Minnie Leigh was collecting her tips and cleaning her last tables before leaving, a familiar voice said, "Excuse me, but I'd like to complain." As Minnie turned to answer the complaint, she found Sadie standing in front of her. Throwing her arms around her and letting out a squeal of joy, she gave Sadie a big hug. Julia was staring at the two friends while cleaning tables close by.

"Well, what's this? One of your family members hiked down the mountain to visit you?"

"No, this is my closest friend, Sadie," Minnie smiled wide. "She lives in Bean Station."

"Well hello, Sadie from Bean Station."

Reaching to take the hand offered her, Sadie shook hands with Julia.

"Well don't just stand there staring at Minnie, let's finish up and take friend Sadie to see the town," Julia suggested.

"Really? I'd love to." Turning to Sadie, Minnie asked, "How about it, Sadie? When're you catching the train back?"

"Have two days. It's all Paw would allow. Yes, I'd love to see the town, I've never seen anything like this place. Not that I'm not excited to see you," Sadie laughed lightly.

Minnie and Julia's boss walked over to see what all the commotion was about.

"Who's this, the Queen of England?"

"No!" Minnie laughed. "This is my closest friend. She came over on the train from Bean Station. Sadie, this is Mr. Callimachi. He's one of the owners and managers of this café."

"Very nice to meet you," he smiled, then turned to Minnie and Julia. "Okay, you two, finish those tables up. And Sadie, what brings you to Knoxville?"

"I came to visit with Minnie, seems she been gone forever."

"Do you ladies have big plans for this visit?"

"I didn't even know she was coming to visit," Minnie said with excitement.

"How long are you going to be here, young lady?"

"Two days."

"Well Minnie, you two can't paint the town up right if you're working," he chuckled, glad to see the girls happy. "You're due some time off. Take two days and show this girl the town."

"That's just what I said," Julia spoke up.

"Take her to a show, show the sights put up on one of those streetcars, she will like that. But *do not* go near that speakeasy! Never know what is going to happen in one of those places."

"What's a speakeasy?" Sadie asked.

"Julia and Minnie will explain it to you," he said with a laugh. "Get going girls, time's a wasting."

Saluting their boss, they skipped out of the café together.

"Julia, my place is closer. We can clean up and change there. I'm sure I have something that'll fit you."

"Thank you. I didn't want to be the only one in a uniform. And it would take too long to go home and get cleaned up there. By the time I got back, the show would be started."

"Before we go too far, let's walk Sadie through the Market House. It won't take long, and I bet she's never seen anything like it."

As they walked through the old building, Sadie couldn't keep her mouth shut. She'd never seen so many vegetables, meats, and other food items.

"Look, Sadie! There's a baker here, Kerns. They have the best bread you've ever eaten."

"People don't make their bread?" Sadie blinked.

Minnie smiled. "No Sadie, people here in the city work, even a lot of the women. So, they come here and can get any baked good they need. You can also give them an order for your favorite pie or cake, and they cook it right up for you. You come back at the assigned time, and it's ready.

"Anyone can rent a space here. It helps farmers, butchers, bakers, dressmakers, candy makers, anyone with wares to sell. It's a place that's dry during the wet season, warm in winter, and out of the heat in the summer."

"They pay money to sell their stuff?"

"It helps because not everyone can afford to build or rent a building to open their shop," Minnie continued.

"During the Civil War, the Union Army, Yankees, occupied Knoxville. The Market House was changed into housing for soldiers. They also stored their ammunition here. There's a huge auditorium on the second floor. A lot of people come here in the evenings to listen to the music. Retired soldiers from every side and every war have meetings there also. At least once a month when they do, the Café is so busy with men folk of all ages, shapes, and sizes."

The girls laughed as they walked back outside to walk Sadie around the outside of the Market House. There were numerous stores to see. As Sadie looked around, she listed the store names in her head. Paw wouldn't believe it. *Market square dry goods, Endicott Johnson Shoe store, The Haynes House, Miller Annex, Steins Diamond Market.*

"Come here Sadie, I want to take you in here." Reading the sign, it said: Robinson Drug Store.

"Minnie, what so unique about a drug store?"

"Just wait, you'll see," Minnie smiled.

Entering, Sadie noticed a marble counter with stools to the left. On the right was a long glass case displaying different items that could be purchased, and at the back of the store was a counter that customers could not see over. There was a gentleman in a white jacket standing behind the counter labeling a

A Mule, A Cow, and 5 Jugs of Shine

dark brown bottle. In the middle of the store, in an elegant row, were marble-topped tables and iron chairs.

"I come here after work sometimes and get me an ice cream soda."

"An ice cream soda?"

"We'll come back and get one before you go home, you won't believe it!"

"Come on girls," Julia cut in. "If we're going to the new theater for a show, we need to go clean up and dress."

"She's right," Minnie nodded.

Walking out of the door and down the street side by side, the girls laughed at Sadie as she pointed at different things. Minnie just smiled, remembering how she had found all of it very strange when she first arrived. She was enjoying reliving that experience through her friend.

As they approached Minnie's apartment building, the streets became crowded.

"What happened to that building?"

"Nothing. Mr. Varner that owns *Minors Department Store* is completing the construction of this building. They say it's going to be a bank."

"He must have a lot of money. Well, that building is big enough to hold all the money in the world!"

"Ha-ha!" Julia laughed. "You'd go *crazy* seeing the buildings where I grew up in New York."

Minnie continued to explain to Sadie about the building they were standing in front of. "The upper rooms are for people that keep track of how much money is deposited there. They also keep track of money for all the businesses in town. Each accountant only takes care of a few business. There're too many for one person to handle."

"I guess that makes sense. Sure is a big building for a bank though."

The girls disappeared into the apartment building.

"I can't believe I'm really here," Sadie said with a wide smile. "It took Miss Betty and Lilly Mae *both* to convince my

113

Paw to let me take the train to see you. Lilly baked pies for me to take him. Every two or three days a week, Miss Betty would send home his favorite meal from the menu the days I worked. She said he was afraid of me missing you so bad, I' find a job here just like you did and never come home."

"My goodness, Sadie, how long have you been planning this trip?" Minnie blinked.

"Since the day you left."

CHAPTER 19

Julia, Minnie, and Sadie walked side by side down the sidewalk, heads erect, backs straight. They were dressed for the show at the new Tennessee Theater. The opening acts were Vaudeville acts, with some local talent mixed in for balance and to help draw the crowd. Tonight's main show would be the first moving picture that Minnie and Sadie had ever seen, and the emotions created between the two friends was washed over in silence.

"Look, you two, you're going to have to quit with the back-home memories," Julia joked. "We're out to have a good time. Don't you hear the music, feel the excitement in the air? Evening time in Knoxville isn't for those whining and pinning over nostalgic memories. We're supposed to be painting the town!"

"You're right, Julia," Minnie nodded. "Where's this theater?"

"Just around the corner."

"Minnie, in all the excitement, I forgot to tell you that Miss Betty said to tell you *hello*, and if you ever get tired of the city, you can have your old job back and your room."

Minnie laughed, but said nothing. The realization that she was still wanted by someone overwhelmed her. But it wasn't Miss Betty she suddenly imagined in her head. It was her Paw with arms outstretched, crying, saying *forgive me.*

Minnie shook her head clear of the picture, and returned her attention to the ticket booth as they approached the theater.

Taking their tickets, they entered the lobby of the newest theater in Knoxville. Even the lobby was a grand sight, everything new. There was the carpet that covered the entire floor and continued up the steps. All three of them were amazed.

"Well, I feel like Cinderella entering the grand palace."

"Minnie, you still make me laugh," Julia teased. "You're like a little girl sometimes. It's like you never in your life could imagine lights that burn without fuel, a mixer to mix flour for cake instead of whipping it by hand, running water, and toilets. Where've you two been? These things aren't new, they've been around forever."

"Julia," Minnie started, "just outside this city, not more than twenty miles are people that still have never dreamed of things like running water and an inside bathroom. I'm sure they're learning as their neighbors update their homes to new fancy ways. Some just don't want to leave their simple life.

"Mountain folks don't want to be like bottomland people. Most of the folk on the mountain are happy. They have an easy life. All they've seen from bottom folk are wars and crime. People took advantage of them, and they see modern inventions as part of the problem. Paw use to say that about *bottom people inventing all kinds of things to make their life easier*. He said it wasn't intended. Idle hands belong to the devil."

"Okay, okay, Minnie," Julia huffed. "Don't get to preaching on mountain people and bottomland people again, calm down. Let's just have a good time and enjoy the show."

The three settled in and soon were laughing and hackling the acts on stage along with the audience, and after the show, they joined another group. Julia had been flirting with one of the young men in the theater, and the girls were invited to join them down by the river for a barn fire.

The group piled into two cars, Minnie and Sadie in one with two overanxious young men, and Julia in the lead car with the other man. Sadie couldn't understand. She told them there was room in their vehicle for more passengers. But by the time they arrived at the riverside, the *why* had become clear.

The two young men in her car were not the brightest bulbs in the lamp. They wore sweaters from the local college and played football. Her guess was intelligence was not required to play college football. She just could not understand how these two could represent a school of pride. She thought only the most intelligent people could get into the University. She had applied herself, and the letter stated though her marks were very high, it was with regret that her admission to University had been turned down. Sadie knew she was smarter than the boy that now stood by her side singing some modern-day song she'd never heard of, "Sonny Boy."

Minnie joined in quickly enough, taking a pull from the jug now and again as it was passed around. Sadie, however, had never partaken of drinking, and was not about to start. Her Paw had taught her that women that drink liquor were not of the proper cloth for marrying. And Sadie was not about to mess up her chances of landing a decent beau.

She watched with mixed feelings as Minnie danced and laughed with the others. It wasn't a side of her friend she'd ever seen before. There was a heaviness and sadness in her heart. It just didn't occur to her at the time that Minnie had been raised very differently than she herself had. She assumed that Minnie's time, though only a little over a year, with Miss Betty had taught her how to behave in public.

Miss Betty was a perfect example of a real lady. She was beautiful, intelligent, and though a widow, she carried herself with dignity and pride. She'd never gone outside the boundaries of what was excepted of a proper lady.

Minnie's behavior was primitive. She'd taken her heels and stockings off right in front of everyone, and was dancing around the fire like some wild native or something. As she passed by Sadie, she held her hands out for Sadie to join in, but Sadie stood her ground.

"What's wrong with your friend?" Julia asked quietly.

"Not sure. We didn't grow up together, so there are some things that strike me strange about her."

"I thought you were best friends?" Julia raised an eyebrow.

"We are. She's the only female friend I've had my whole life. Well, there's Miss Betty, but she's more like a mother to me. I've only known them for a little over a year. See Julia, I'm the one that's the hillbilly, not Sadie. So, from now on, don't speak to her as you did earlier. There's nothing I would not do to protect her."

With that, Minnie walked over to where the jug was and took another long draw from it, then let out a blood-curdling yell like none of them have ever heard. Julia looked on with a new realization of her new friend. She realized that Minnie was no dumb hillbilly. She was intelligent beyond her years and devoted too, as deep as the roots that held the mountains to the earth.

The young men insisted on taking their new female companions back to town. "Coach would fry us if we were the cause of a local girl getting into trouble of any kind." Minnie and Julia laughed at this.

The two were surprisingly steady on their feet, and able to climb out of the car with minimal help. As Minnie took the hand of her
'footman,' she swung him around and started dancing right there on the sidewalk.

"Minnie Leigh!" Sadie yelled like a mother scolding a child.

Instead of everyone turning to see what Minnie was doing, it was Sadie that eyes bored through right now. Embarrassed and exasperated with tonight's events, Sadie ran into the apartment house, straight up the steps, and waited by the door.

She forgot all about the boys, and running up the stairs and toward her friend, Minnie didn't understand what she'd done that had upset her friend.

"Come on Sadie, tell me what's wrong. You seem very upset. I didn't mean nothin' by dancing with him. Just joshin'. I'm sure it's you he likes, all he says is *Sadie this, Sadie that...*"

Minnie tried to explain.

"What're you *talking* about Minnie? You, just now howling like a banshee. *That's* what I'm upset about! Now can we go in our room and discuss this? It's not everyone's business," Sadie snapped.

"Whatever makes you happy."

The girls entered the room.

"Now Sadie, can you please explain what in the world has you so upset?"

"*You*," Sadie narrowed her eyes. "You're acting like…I don't know what. A lady doesn't go stripping her shoes and stockings off in public, and you surely don't drink like menfolk in public. A lady doesn't drink hard liquor at all!"

"Why? Sadie, why doesn't a lady drink hard liquor?"

Sadie looked shocked at the question, and realized she didn't know why. She just knew her Paw had taught her not to drink because she was a proper lady.

"Well Minnie, I'm not sure why," Sadie admitted, but continued to stand her ground. "But Paw has always told me that a lady doesn't drink hard liquor. Besides, the way you were acting *scared* me."

"Sadie, it's good you have a Paw that loves you. He teaches you the things he thinks is best for you. But I come from a different place, and our ways are different. I can't think of one thing I did tonight that I should be ashamed of. I'm learning, and if one day I see that I'm wrong, I'll say so. But right now, I don't see where I'm wrong."

"I'm sorry we disagree Minnie, but ladies should *never* act the way you did tonight. Maybe acting loose and wild is okay in the mountains, but not here," Sadie finished.

With that, the girls all changed for bed. Laying there in her bed, Minnie Leigh wondered where her behavior really came from. She still didn't feel ashamed of anything she did. Was Sadie right, should she be? Julia had not said anything this whole time. Checking, Minnie found she was fast asleep.

When Minnie woke up, it was much later than she was

used to. It was daylight out. She knew without looking Julia was already gone. She had to be at the café early this morning. Turning to wake Sadie to start their day, Minnie saw the bed was empty. Her heart sank for a moment, but she decided Sadie must be down the hall using the facilities.

After a sufficient amount of time, Minnie, now dressed, opened the door and went down the hall to check. Coming back into her room, she scanned around. Then she noticed Sadie's night bag was gone.

Grabbing her pocketbook and locking the door behind her, Minnie ran as fast as she could to the train station. It seemed like the ground under her was moving, but she was getting nowhere. She hit the depot doors with such force, several passengers waiting jumped with a start. She ran to the ticket counter, and tried to see the boarding platform at the same time.

"Has the train for Johnson City left?" Minnie asked.

The startled ticket master, with his mouth agape, pointed as the train was pulling away from the platform. Minnie sprinted to the door, but was left standing there with tears streaming down her face, watching the last passenger car windows speed past as the train gained momentum.

When Minnie walked through the café doors dressed to work, and without Sadie, Julia said nothing. And when Mr. Callimachi started toward her, Julia held out her arm, looked at him, shook her head, and said, "Not yet, let her be for now."

They both watched as Minnie came straight in, put a smile on her face, and started clearing the dirty tables. She chatted with customers, and laughed at a few jokes. The smile never left her face, and if you didn't know her, you'd never be able to tell her heart was in shreds over Sadie.

CHAPTER 20

Minnie glided through a few days following Sadie's visit. Today she was walking through the park. She liked this place even though there were usually a fair amount of people walking the footpaths. It was peaceful, almost like a church.

Her heart was broken still, over Sadie being disappointed in her, and there had been no return letter. Maybe there hadn't been enough time to receive one yet. She didn't know. Finding a bench off the main path, Minnie Leigh sat down to gather her thoughts.

"God, it's Minnie Leigh. You might not remember me. It's been so long since I spoke to you. I've never thanked you for my new home, my job, and good friends. It's not any of the new stuff that's a botherin' me, though. It's Sadie. She's my closest friend I ever had. She's all mad at me.

"Here it is. Now, when I lived at home, Paw always passed the jug to me. Now, he wouldn't let me drink as he did, but never had to. I was young, didn't take much. And when there was music or a barn fire, we all danced. What seems to be the problem? I don't understand why she's so upset. Even not drinkin', I feel like dancing a lot of times. Just don't understand why I can't just be *me*. If'n you'in can help me with this one, please. My heart's hurting awful bad."

Minnie set quietly on the park bench for a long time, expecting God to answer somehow. She didn't know what she expected; a hand delivered answer from him? Maybe a preacher to walk up and say, "Minnie Leigh, God said—"

Laughing at herself, she stood. "I must be crazy to think

God would answer me. What I ever do that he'd speak to me?"

Shaking her head and laughing at herself, she walked back toward the square.

When Minnie was crossing the lobby in her apartment house, the Landlord yelled for her, letting her know there was mail for her. Anxious to see if Sadie had responded, she grabbed the letters. There wasn't a letter from Sadie. However, there was one from Miss Betty.

Dear Minnie,

I hope this letter finds you well. I am sorry your visit with Sadie did not go as planned. She told me what happened. I don't want you to feel bad though, you come from a different life, and she does not understand. I am sure you will find your way. Keep being yourself, don't neglect your time alone. Greet the morning as you always have. Talk to God. He will show you the way. We all miss you and love you. Work hard, come home when you can.

Love,
Betty

The letter was a comfort to Minnie, though she would have preferred one from her friend. How simple her life might be if she'd remained in the mountains. Living in the mountains seemed like so long ago and far away. She couldn't believe it had already been two years, almost three, since she walked away from everything she'd ever known. Minnie was glad to be living on her own, but who *was* she? What kind of person would she become? She'd never thought past being a wife and mother, living out her days in the east Tennessee mountains. Minnie never thought that becoming educated and learning a trade would also change her.

As her thoughts wandered back and forth, Minnie realized that maybe it wasn't the liquor, the dancing, or even her wild nature that was the problem. Perhaps it was just the place, the timing. Would it ever be okay for her to express herself as she had growing up? Sort of wild, free? Did becoming older, a grown city woman, mean she could never again revisit those things that she saw as her roots, her foundation? Was every part of her heritage a bad thing?

Minnie dressed for work. As she walked through the people and sights that had become so familiar to her, she felt there was a change coming. She felt like she was being prepared for something that would not be easy. Her intuition caused her to hold onto and almost completely hoard every nickel she made.

One day as she was serving her regular customers, a group of people came through the doors with much commotion. There were about eight people in the party. They were all dressed in very fancy clothes, their coats all had fur around the neck. The females in the party had make-up on, and carried themselves like they were just a little better than the next person.

Mr. Callimachi and Mr. Kallergis both walked over to the group, taking their coats and hanging them up, pulling tables together, and arranging them where they weren't too close to the other customers. There was much to do with these customers, more than Minnie had ever seen. One of the older servers were assigned to assist the two owners as they took orders.

Shortly after they were settled in and drinks served, Minnie noticed one of the cooks that often ran out for unique ingredients went running out of the door toward the Market House with a list in hand. Once he returned, the two owners were seen in the kitchen cooking up the food. They didn't often help out. Undoubtedly, this group must be *somebody* because all care was taken to get everything just right.

"Hey, Julia who're these people? Mr. Callimachi and Mr. Kallergis are putting on the dog for them."

"See the lady sitting on the other side of the table closest to the window? That's Grace Moore, you should've heard of her. She is just like you," Julia raised her eyebrows. "She walked out of the mountain. She's from Slabtown Tennessee or something like that. She's known as the "Tennessee Nightingale" 'cause she sings opera. She's also starred in a couple of moving pictures. There's talk that she's the greatest female singer that ever has been."

"You don't say?" Minnie said slowly. "And she walked out of the mountain just like me?"

"Well not exactly, I believe she moved with her parents. Her father's a preacher or something. Saying goes, her parents weren't happy about her wanting to be a singer."

Without a word, Minnie Leigh walked over to the table straight to Miss Moore's side. The owners and Julia looked on with horror, knowing that this might not be good. As Miss Moore stood up, they all held their breath, not knowing what to except. What happened next took them all by surprise.

They watched in astonishment as Miss Moore wrapped her arms around Minnie Leigh, hugging her tight just as if she was a long-lost sister. There were tears and everything. Miss Moore returned to her seat, and asked for a piece of paper and something to write with.

As Minnie returned to the counter where Julia was, everyone just stared at her. Minnie just had a huge smile, but a look of amazement on her face.

After what seemed forever Julia said, "Well?"

"Well, what?"

"You know what!" Julia's eyes widened. "You didn't know who she was and next thing I know, you two are hugging and crying like you were long-lost relatives."

"She might as well be," Minnie smiled knowingly. "See, there's one thing city folk will never understand: mountain people are connected. We're connected in such a way that none other will ever understand."

"I guess," was all Julia could say.

As the group stood to leave, Grace Moore crossed the room to where Minnie was cleaning a table. She handed her a piece of paper, hugged her again, and told her she would see her later. With that, she gathered her coat from one of her companions, and left. The whole time, she was looking over her shoulder at Minnie with a look of longing, like she didn't want to leave Minnie behind. Minnie Leigh nodded her head, and waved good-bye.

As Julia and Minnie were hanging their aprons on the pegs in the back room preparing to leave, Julia asked Minnie if she'd like to join her and some friends at the Bijou.

"I have plans this evening," Minnie smiled.

"You do? New beau?" Julia raised an eyebrow.

"No," is all Minnie Leigh would say.

Minnie almost ran home.

She ran into her room, laying out all her dresses, four of them, and the one pair of heels she owned. She tore out of her room without locking the door, and dashed into the indoor facilities. She had nothing but lye soap, so it would have to do. She turned the water on and didn't even wait for it to warm, it took too long. She climbed in and started bathing as quick as she could, dried, threw her house dress back on, ran back to the room, and after much debate, chose a dress. She pulled on a pair of silk stockings she was saving for a special occasion, but she didn't think her overcoat was proper enough. Though the evening air was cool, she decided not to wear it.

Arriving at the Andrew Johnson Hotel, Minnie found a grand entrance hall. There was a very high, open ceiling with balconies that overlooked the lobby. There was also a grand staircase. As she started to walk toward the desk, she heard a female voice across the lobby calling her name.

"Minnie! Over here."

When she looked in the direction of the voice, she saw Grace descending the last few steps of the staircase.

Walking over with purposeful grace in her steps, Minnie and Grace embraced again like old friends.

"Hello, Miss Grace," Minnie beamed.

But Grace shook her head. "Not Miss, just Grace."

"Okay."

"Minnie dear, you're freezing. Where's your overcoat?"

"I don't have one that was proper enough to wear," Minnie shrugged.

"Minnie, you don't ever have to worry about being *proper* around me," Grace said with kind eyes. "We're cut from the same cloth, dear."

"I just didn't want to be an embarrassment to you, ma'am."

"Minnie, learn now to be who you are. Grant it, there are things we have to change to be excepted in public, but never lose who you are. It's part of our public appeal. People in general are so enthralled that you come from *backwoods* and are educated and talented," Grace reminded Minnie." Come, lets us find a place to sit and talk. The hotel itself isn't complete inside, and there aren't many guests, but there's exceptions when you're *somebody*."

Finding an area where there was a couple of couches and chairs arranged for lounging, Minnie and Grace took a seat.

Sitting next to Minnie, Grace Moore took Minnie's hands in hers. "Minnie, you're a breath of fresh air. Now tell me why and how you left your mountain home."

Minnie launched right in, starting with a brief history of her immediate family, then skipping to the place where her Paw traded her to Tolbert. She told the story in great detail. Grace was moved, and even shed tears at times. Minnie shared her story right up to the point where she met Miss Moore at the café.

"My goodness, Minnie. Yours is a story that's made to move all others to the point of encouragement. Tell me what your plans are."

"My only plans are to make a good living hopefully, meet a man worth marrying, raise my children to know mountain ways, but to be educated and successful."

"There's no doubt in my mind that you'll do just that, Minnie. When I was young, I sang in my family's church, and everyone was always telling me I sang like a bird. I never quit singing. My father moved us to Knoxville, which was awful. He later moved us to Jellico where I finished school. I moved to Nashville for college, then to New York where I got my first paying job singing at the *Black Cat Café*. From there, I kept working hard and tried out for a Broadway play. All history from there. There have been many jobs, and I've grown and enjoyed each one of them.

"Once in a while, I slip home just to feel grounded. I usually stay in Knoxville or somewhere close. It hasn't changed much, though it seems to be trying. Still a little crass, but I'm sure Knoxville will one day be remembered as a grand place. It's just how east Tennessee is., always striving to make better." Grace's expression grew sad. "I'll be leaving in two days for Paris. So, it was important that I met with you tonight."

"My goodness," Minnie said breathless, just as if she'd been the one talking. "Grace, you've lived one heck of a life."

"That I have, Minnie, and it all started with a love for the song. So, find what it is you love and never quit."

"The thing I love the most is the idea of a strong family. A husband that is, a good father that loves his children, especially his girls. All I want is to feel wanted, safe, and protected. I think that's enough. It is for me anyways."

"I say it is, Minnie, if that's what's in your heart. We all have our place in the world, and strong families are part of what makes our country a great place. My father raised us to be assured that God isn't surprised at the paths we choose. Walk it with Him. and walk it steady, that's all that's important," Grace smiled wide.

"I'm so glad we met, Grace. It's like I've met a sister that I never knew."

"It's the same for me, Minnie. But...before you go, I have something for you. Stay here, I'll be right back." Getting up and ascending the grand staircase, Grace returned shortly with a beautiful overcoat trimmed with a fur collar. "This is for you, so you never have to feel you're an embarrassment to anyone."

"Oh, my! Oh, my goodness!" Minnie's eyes widened. "Are you *sure?*"

"As sure as I've ever been about anything."

The two ladies embraced again, this time lingering as if they knew they would never see each other again.

CHAPTER 21

Before you knew it, October and November had passed, bringing in the Christmas season and another year. Soon it would be 1929, and three and a half years since Minnie had left her mountain on the adventure that would become her life.

Christmas and New Year's passed with a flurry of celebrations. Minnie went to Bean Station for a brief visit, bringing with her gifts and stories of failures and success. The evening before she left to return to Knoxville, Sadie came into the café.

"Well, I thought I'd never see you," Minnie's expression softened. "Betty said you still worked here, so I was waiting to surprise you when you came to work."

"I heard you were coming to town and I had full intention of not working until you left," Sadie admitted. But her face was genuine. "But we're friends, and I shouldn't hold on to bad feelings.

"Minnie, I want to say I'm sorry for being so mad at you. I didn't and still don't understand your ways. But no matter how different we are, or how much we disagree, you're my dearest friend, and I love you no matter what," she finished with a smile.

"Sadie, I'm so glad you feel that way," Minnie let out a breath. "I couldn't bear the thought of never talking with you again. I love you too, and always want the best for you. If I'm not the best friend for you, I'll stay away."

"Don't you dare stay away! You better plan on coming home as often as you can, and I'll come to Knoxville as much as I can. Agree?"

"Agreed!"

The two friends sat for hours after opening each other's gifts, drinking coffee. Minnie told Sadie about meeting the great Grace Moore and all the other adventures, lessons, and mistakes she'd made.

Sadie shared about almost being engaged, but that she thought better of it when she found out her intended helped sell shine for his Paw occasionally. The next morning, it was Sadie that saw Minnie off at the train station. At last, Minnie felt a complete peace again. She waved, knowing they were both okay.

The year passed much like the last. Julia had met a gentleman and was planning a wedding. They spent time sitting around talking about where they'd live and how many kids they'd have, though Julia's husband-to-be did not want her working. This would be a significant change, but she was excited. Minnie was once again being left alone as life and friendships changed, as lives grew independent of each other.

Minnie was thinking about moving to Dallas. She'd heard that it was still a town finding its way, but had great potential. There were plans for building several new high-rise hotels. However, there was the question of "The Market." Would American finances remain stable as the country planned for its moving into another decade? 1930 was fast approaching.

Minnie had been listening to the talk of how Texas had pulled ahead of all other oil-rich states to become the top producer of crude oil, providing sixty percent of all oil and fuel in America. The more she heard of Texas, and especially Dallas, the more she started thinking, and remembered how Grace Moore told her to always to follow the dream of her heart.

She began to plan. She'd ask questions of anyone that mentioned Texas. Those that spoke of Texas, but had never been there, she cut short in conversation. It was the customers and strangers on the street that she met in passing conversation that had been there, lived there, and knew what it was like that she sought out.

Some grew suspicious of her intense questioning. What was this gal up to?

Minnie counted and re-counted her money, making sure she had train fare from Knoxville, Tennessee, to Memphis, and from Memphis to Dallas, Texas. She was excited that she would pass through other towns that she'd often heard of, but she had no intention of getting off the train except to board a connecting train until she reached her destination in Dallas.

As September turned into October, strong talk and political unrest were surrounding the stability of the country. One day, as Minnie and the other servers cleared tables after the lunch crowd, the owners went running from the offices upstairs out of the café.

"Now what do you suppose they're up in arms about?"

"There's no telling. Maybe they had a word of someone trying to buy the first load of fall vegetables again."

Soon, someone came into the café flustered and asked the girls if they had heard the news.

"What news?" Minnie asked.

"The market's crashing! Banks are starting to fail everywhere!"

Most of the girls pulled their aprons off, throwing them to the table, and went running out the door. Minnie was stunned, and didn't know what to do.

Shortly the owners came walking back in.

"Minnie, you might as well leave with the rest of them. Go check your bank. You need to see if you've lost all your savings."

Minnie slowly removed her apron, and began to feel thankful that something had told her to start hiding money in containers around her room. She was even more grateful that she hadn't been robbed as of yet.

As she entered the bank building, there were many patrons full of concern. She overheard some saying the bank had not yet received word of their plight in the Market disaster. It was October the 24th, 1929.

Minnie stepped to the window for her turn to inquire about her deposits. As the teller started to explain that her money was still safe, "so far," Minnie decided on the spur of the moment to withdraw her entire savings.

"Please, may a have my savings in cash? I'd like to close my account."

"Ma'am, if you'll wait just a few days, we're confident that the Market will right itself."

"That's very nice to hear. But my withdrawing my money has nothing to do with the market. I'm leaving town, and I require my full savings to make a move."

"Ma'am, again, we assure you if you could just wait a day or so..."

"You see though, I'll be leaving in the morning. I don't have a couple of days. So, if you'll be kind enough to give me my savings in cash, I'll be closing my account."

With reluctance, the teller gathered Minnie's money and placed it in a bag. Minnie slipped the bag under her blouse and folded her arms around her waist. She went straight to her apartment house.

Minnie stood in the middle of the room. Not believing how fast things were happening, she pulled her suit case out from under the bed, carefully packed it, placing her bag of money in the bottom under her clothes. Next, she removed the jars and containers of money she had hidden all in her room. There were eight of them, she couldn't believe her eyes.

Once she bagged it all up and then checked the room once more, she donned the over coat gifted to her by Miss Grace, and headed for the café for the last time.

When she entered the door, the owners stood there bewildered as they had already lost four girls, including Julia.

"Not you too."

"Well, I've been planning, and with all that's happing today, I decided on the spur of the moment that today is as good a time as any to go ahead and leave for Dallas."

Hugging her ever so tightly, the owners wished her well.

They told her if she ever needed a work reference, they would be glad to wire it to her new employer. Minnie picked up her suit case, and headed for the train station. After purchasing her ticket to Memphis, she stepped out onto the train platform to wait for the train that should arrive shortly.

She set her suitcase down and used it for a seat. Minnie was very nervous, knowing that everything and every dime she owned was inside that suitcase. She would not be letting it out of her sight.

Just as she got comfortable, the train pulled in. Minnie didn't bother moving until most of the passengers had parted the train. She then stood, picked up her suitcase, and boarded the train. She found a seat, and prayed the empty one beside her remained that way.

After a short wait, the train whistle sounded a warning, and then there was the familiar cry: "*All aboard! Passengers, all aboard!*"

Minnie began to feel excited about what she would find in Dallas. After about an hour out, she began to get comfortable, and her day dreams subsided. The conductor passed thru checking and punching tickets.

"Ma'am, we can put your luggage in the luggage car if you'd like."

"No thank you," Minnie said. "I prefer to keep it with me."

"Okay. If you change your mind, I assure you it'll be safe locked in there. We have armed guards in the luggage car."

Minnie held her suitcase tight against the foot of the seat with her legs.

As early morning turned into mid-day, the conductor came through checking on the passengers. Stopping at Minnie Leigh's side, he informed her that she could now purchase a meal in the dining car. Minnie thanked him.

She realized she was hungry. Opening her bag, she removed the paper sack that was packed for her at The Golden Sun Café as she departed Knoxville. In the sack were three sandwiches, cake, and cheese. The girls at the café had told Minnie they packed her a snack. There was enough food in the sack to last her all the way to Dallas. Minnie would miss her friends in Knoxville, but felt very confident in her choice to move to Dallas with its steady economy.

CHAPTER 22

After seven days of traveling on one train and then another, Minnie felt she'd been tossed back and forth enough to last a life time. As she stepped off the train in Dallas, she knew that she'd made the right choice. But as she walked around the depot building, she stopped dead still.

"Oh my, I didn't send Miss Betty a telegram or letter letting her know I left Knoxville. I have to remember to write as soon as I find a room."

Minnie quickly found that the train station was centrally located. Later, she found out that the city's early planners had designed this on purpose. Having the train station close to the city center helped to distribute materials and export products easily.

After walking a few blocks toward the city center and asking a few street vendors, Minnie was directed to an apartment house. She was very pleased to find that the apartment was clean, and had a separate room for sleeping. She'd never known such a place existed. After looking over the available rooms, she chose one that had a view of the city. She also could not believe that her room was ten stories above street level.

She divided her money, paying for three months in advance. As promised by the front desk help, the rest of her money was locked in a safe right there in the building. Minnie felt it would be safer there than in a bank.

Unlike her first experience when moving to Knoxville, this time she had money, and was able to choose an apartment to her liking and not just for shelter. Her room also had a private bathroom. No more sharing a shower and tub with everyone in the building.

She carefully unpacked and hung her dresses. Next, she drew a hot bath and took her time bathing. Dressed in her house dress, she settled on the couch and opened the newspaper she had bought after arriving in the city. As she read, she began feeling reassured this move was the right for her.

Dallas was not expected to suffer any effect due to the overall bank failure in America. Marion Joiner struck oil a hundred miles east of Dallas in Kilgore, spawning the east Texas oil boom. Dallas was quickly becoming the financial center for the oil industry in Texas and Oklahoma. Banks were making loans to develop the oil fields, and Dallas was becoming a financial center for the east Texas industry. This put off most thoughts of depression.

As she read on, reports from Tennessee, Mississippi, Alabama, and South Carolina were very dismal. Nashville and Knoxville were mentioned in the article as well. Four out of every five people previously employed were without work as businesses had to close their doors or cut back to survive.

Thinking again of Miss Betty, Minnie Leigh quickly dressed and grabbed her purse. Stopping briefly at the front desk, she got direction for the nearest telegraph office, realizing that a telegram would reach Bean Station faster than a posted letter. She was willing to pay the extra money to assure her friend she was okay, and had made the last-minute decision to move on to Texas: *Miss Betty...stop...I am ok...stop...Moved to Dallas...stop...Letter to follow...stop...Love Minnie Leigh...stop.*

After sending the Telegram, Minnie walked the streets, not really looking for anything, but admiring her surroundings. Reminiscing, she thought about her journey, coming out of the mountain, and Miss Betty rescuing her. She'd formed a new life in Bean Station and discovered a new family. She'd had no intention of ever leaving Knoxville, and Dallas was only a place that she wanted to visit not move to. Fear had overcome her the day she fled Tennessee, the same kind of fear that had gripped her when she fled the mountain. She wanted to live, to survive. Somewhere in her seemed to be this force that caused her to just run, run to somewhere new.

Refocusing on her surroundings, she felt alone. There was no one here. In Tennessee, she could board a train and within a couple of hours, be in Bean Station with Miss Betty, Sadie, Lilly Mae, and Joe. There were people there she loved. How were they surviving? Was the financial crisis affecting them?

Minnie had left town on October 24th. Five days later on the 29th was the day newspapers heralded: *"TOTAL BANK COLLAPSE: AMEREICA has plunged into the GREAT DEPRESSION."*

Minnie crossed the street and was looking up at the sheer size of some of the buildings when she heard the clatter of dishes, and had a whiff of a familiar aroma. Looking across the street, she saw no sign of a dinner, café, or restaurant, and looking down the street in front of her, there was no signs advertising eateries of any kind. She did notice a group of people chatting away turn into the tall building in front of her. She decided to follow them, having the feeling that where there was a group of people, there was usually food involved.

She followed them into a great, open lobby. Just a short distance to the left, there it was: tables scattered in formation, covered in fine white table clothes, and dishes properly set out at each seat awaiting customers.

Minnie smoothed her dress, pulled her gloves tight, straightened her back, and worked slowly and purposely up to the hostess stand.

"Yes, may I help you? Do you have a lunch reservation?"

"No," Minnie answered. "I'd like to inquire about employment."

Looking her up and down as if he were the one that would decide, the gentleman paused, then asked her to follow him. They weaved through the tables, pushed through the swing doors into the kitchen, making a sharp left they arrived at an office door bearing a sign that read *"Adolphus Hotel: Restaurant Manager."*

Knocking twice, then opening the door, the gentleman stepped in, and Minnie followed. "This young lady, Miss—?" he hesitated, realizing he had forgotten to obtain her name.

Stepping up, she held out her hand to the distinguished older woman behind the desk "Minnie Leigh Robertson. I am inquiring about employment. I have experience as a cook and server. I have references if you require them. I am dependable, willing to work anytime, and stay until the job is complete."

Minnie spoke clearly and directly, not wanting to give this lady a chance to tell her there was no work.

Relaxing back in her chair and smiling, the Manager began sizing Minnie up. "Now, where in the world do you get an accent like that one? It's the most melonic accent I've ever heard. It's like you are singing a slow southern ballet. Tell me girl, where're you from?"

"Ma'am, I'm from east Tennessee, as far and as high as it goes. My mountain touches the mountains of North Carolina and Virginia."

"*Your* mountain? You own a mountain?" she slowly raised an eyebrow.

"Well no ma'am, that is how we say it when describing our home. If you were born there, it's a part of you, and you're a part of it. Just like Miss Grace Moore and I were saying, no one could understand unless you're from there."

"You know Grace Moore, the movie star? The greatest female vocalist ever?" The woman couldn't believe what she was hearing.

"Yes ma'am, we're from the same mountain. Well originally, her folks moved her off when she was a young girl."

"Then how do you know her? You're so much younger than she is."

"Well before she went to Paris, she was in *The Gold Sun Café* in Knoxville," Minnie explained with a shrug.

"Oh, and you think because you waited on her or something you are now best friends," the woman huffed, squaring her shoulders. "Young lady, I'll tell you up front, I don't like people that take a smidgen of fact and create wild tales."

"No ma'am, it's not a wild tale," she shook her head. "We also had a visit at her motel later that day. We sat for hours talking. She told me about her journey out of the mountain, and what her life has been like since. She even gave me one of her over coats with a fur collar."

"Did she now?" the woman hummed. "That remains to be seen."

"Oh, you'll see it ma'am. But I only wear it when there's a good chill in the air, and if'n I not working."

"Do you now?" she hummed louder. "Well, Miss Robertson..."

"Just Minnie, if you please."

"Okay, *just Minnie*..."

"No ma'am, Minnie. Not *just Minnie*," Minnie raised an eyebrow.

Smiling, the Manager tried not to laugh at this simple young girl that clearly didn't understand sarcasm. "I'll give you a trial period. I'll start you in the kitchen, and if you do well there, we'll see about letting you serve the customers. In the meantime, you bring in your reference letters for me to look over. Can you start tomorrow?"

"Yes, yes, ma'am, I'd be glad too. How early would you like me to be here? Four, maybe five am?"

"Four AM?!" The Manager was shocked at the thought. "The restaurant doesn't even open until eight AM."

"Eight AM! How on earth do the guests get their breakfast before work?"

"Work? Minnie our guests are here visiting," the Manager sighed a bit. "Some of them are office workers, then there are the ones that have apartments here just to stay in when they're in town checking on their oil holdings. This is no *backwoods* town."

"No ma'am, I didn't mean anything. It's just the last place I worked never closed," Minnie tried to explain. "It was in downtown Knoxville near the Market House. People came and went all hours of the day and night."

"Yes, well, you'll find our clientele is quite different. You'll report to work at noon tomorrow. Meet me here, and I'll show you around and find you a uniform."

"I'll be here." Minnie quickly left the room before the Manager could change her mind.

"Now if I didn't know better, I'd think that lady was making fun of me."

Putting the interview out of her mind, Minnie walked out of the building and through the city blocks, completely amazed at the sheer size of the buildings. Once again, Minnie had secured a job, and begun a new life.

CHAPTER 23

1930 arrived without much fanfare for Minnie. She continued to work in the kitchen of the Adolphus Hotel, mainly washing dishes and bussing tables. Occasionally, she carried trays to the table for the servers of elite clientele. It was all designed to give the guests assurance that they were the best of society, and the Adolphus was the place to stay and eat if you weren't just anyone. Minnie thought the over-exaggerated gesture was ridiculous, and was sure one day the hotel would have to open its doors to anyone that would pay.

As the year waned on into April, the effects of the Great Depression started to take a toll on Dallas. The whole state of Texas had fared well to this point due to the overwhelming boom in the oil industry. But with the passing of time, more and more people were put out of work, and less and less could afford to keep their cars and trucks, much less fuel them. It all took a toll on petroleum profits. Whatever affected the petroleum industry affected Dallas.

Bookings at the Adolphus Hotel fell off, and so did the guests at the restaurant. Some of the kitchen staff moved west thinking that as the movie industry grew, and Los Angeles became a focal town, that like Dallas, it would be protected against the effects of the Depression.

Minnie was promoted by default.

The Manager had been holding her back, though she had received her letters of recommendation, only seeing Minnie as a young, unintelligent girl. Maybe she did have talent at serving, but that hillbilly talk had to go.

Yet as staff became shorter and shorter, Minnie began taking on extra tasks. She didn't ask. If she saw something that was being neglected, she just simply stepped in and took care of it. She could usually figure out how to repair a kitchen appliance with relative ease.

One day mid-afternoon, Minnie, as she finished bussing a table, noticed several place settings that were askew. She wiped her hands on a damp towel hanging from her waist, and dried them on the tail of her apron. She carefully straightened the table cloth without touching the top services. Next, she placed her finger tips on the underneath of the plate rims and made the appropriate adjustments. She had not noticed the gentleman sitting quietly at the table along the wall.

"May I ask why you took such care when you touched that plate just now?"

"Well, even though I know my hands are relatively clean, I just thought how I wouldn't want someone putting their hands all over my plate."

"Are you one of my servers?" he watched her.

"No sir, I was hired to work in the kitchen. I have excellent references, but I don't think the manager likes me very well," Minnie admitted with a shrug. "I have a notion she thinks I'm not very intelligent. But during these times, I have no complaint. I'm working and living in a good city."

After a couple seconds, Minnie noticed the gentleman didn't even have a glass of water yet. Walking a few steps to the server's station, Minnie poured him a glass of water, and placed it on the table in front of him.

"Sir, has anyone taken your order? You must've been sitting here for a while. I didn't see you when I came in to clear the tables."

"No, no they haven't," he smiled.

"What can I get you?"

"What are you specials today?"

Even though Minnie was not a server she always knew what the specials were. She memorized the weekly special menu. She'd started this practice when she was hired. Every week, the Chef would change at least one special for the week. Minnie checked in the morning to see if it was something different. From time to time while cleaning tables, a customer that didn't want to take time to read the menu would ask her what the specials were. After the first time not knowing, she made it a point to be prepared. Minnie rattled off the specials and their prices.

"Well, I'll like to have the corn beef sandwich special, and a fresh cup of coffee," he nodded.

"Coming right up."

As Minnie turned, there suddenly stood the Manager. "Just what do you think you're *doing?*" the woman narrowed her eyes.

"Whatever I see that needs to be done, miss," Minnie stated matter-of-factly. "Right now, I'm taking this gentleman's order because no one has even bothered to greet him or give him a simple glass of water."

"Minnie, you simpleton. Do you not know who this *is?*" the Manager's eyes widened.

Before Minnie could turn around to look at him again, the gentleman put his finger to his mouth. Looking at the Manager, he motioned for her to not say anything. Minnie took a long look, and turned back around.

"No ma'am, he doesn't look like anyone I know. He does, however, look like a customer who might like his food before bedtime tonight. So, if you'll excuse me, I'm going to go and put his order in."

Walking around her manager and picking up her tub of dirty dishes, Minnie went into the kitchen and put in the order for the gentleman's sandwich.

"If that girl isn't one of our servers, she should be. She should be your assistant. I sat here and in less than five minutes, I could tell this young lady was not doing the job she should be," he huffed at the Manager.

"What did she do wrong?" the Manager asked in exasperation. "How could she mess up cleaning dirty dishes from a table?"

"That's the thing, she did nothing wrong," he smiled. "She cleaned the table, then noticed a place setting was out of line and fixed it. Then she was upset when she realized no one had bothered to serve me."

While they were still talking, Minnie Leigh delivered his food. She had straightened her hair and put on a clean apron. Then she retrieved a pitcher of cold water and refilled his glass.

"Do you require anything else now, sir?"

"No, thank you miss," he continued to smile.

With that, Minnie retreated to her station in the kitchen.

"I want this young girl trained in all aspects of the restaurant, she'll be your new assistant," the gentleman waved his hand toward the Manager with a wider smile, and dismissed her without a word.

The Manager went to Minnie first. "Minnie Leigh, report to work in the morning at eight AM instead of your regular time. You may clock out now." Then entering her office, she slammed the door and locked it.

Minnie quickly pulled her apron off, gathered her things, and walked out through the dining room. The gentleman was no longer sitting at the table, but he'd left Minnie a tip. It was one of the largest she'd ever received.

"God, you're amazing. I never know when you're going to step in and change things for me. Thank you."

Minnie was very aware that because of the instruction from Miss Betty on money and preparing for tough times, she herself had not realized the extreme effects of The Depression as so many had. So, Minnie volunteered for soup lines and distributed clothes. In the less fortunate areas of town, Minnie tended to the sick, and tutored children. She tried her best to encourage and leave them hopeful.

Despite training for Assistant Manager and doing well, Minnie continued to wash dishes, wait tables, and keep the dining room in top shape. She was supposed to take over ordering food and reviewing the books after the Manager as a double check for any mistakes too. However, the manager always kept her from the books, and kept them locked up.

Then one day, Minnie knocked on the door and walked in. There was no one there, and the books were laid open on the desk. She walked around and looked at them. She wanted to see what was so hard about adding and subtracting numbers that her manager kept putting off that part of her training. Odd enough, there were two set of books. Minnie scanned one and then the other, trying to understand how it worked.

She did notice they were almost identical, except one had added pay-outs for things like a new cooler for the kitchen, repair on the stoves, and plumbing repairs. She needed to ask where these things were. Maybe they were trying to see if the restaurant could afford the work. It didn't set right with her.

As she was leaving the office, the Manager was approaching. "Did you need something?"

"No. I placed some invoices on your desk and was going to let you know I was finished for the day."

"Very well," the Manager huffed, and vanished.

Minnie didn't know why she didn't mention the books.

It had become a habit to walk home instead of taking a street car. No matter how long she was on her feet, the walking calmed her, made her feel better. She crossed the street and a few blocks down, entered her favorite bakery. She would buy her bread and sweet cakes here.

Standing at the counter in front of her was a very well-dressed couple. She thought the gentleman was familiar, and when they turned to go, he saw her. It was the gentleman she had waited on at the restaurant.

"Well hello, young lady, how're you doing?" the smiled.

"I'm fine, thank you."

"This is my wife, Alice," he gestured to the pretty woman standing beside him.

Bowing her head slightly, she held out her hand. "My name's Minnie Leigh Robertson. I had the pleasure to serve your husband one day at the *Adolphus Hotel* restaurant."

"Pleased to meet you," the woman smiled, almost knowingly. "Yes, he must check on many of the family's businesses. It makes it very easy having an apartment upstairs."

"Oh," Minnie blinked. "I didn't realize you owned the restaurant."

"Well, I didn't want to make you nervous," he chuckled. "You were tired, and the Manager seemed to be giving you a hard time even though you were just doing what you thought was best. How're you liking your new position? Have you learned much?"

Minnie shrugged. "To tell the truth, I'm still doing the same things I was doing: washing dishes, waiting tables. She keeps saying she's going to explain the bookkeeping to me, but she just closes the books up and locks them in her desk draw." Then Minnie remembered. "I did get a look at them today, but she wasn't there to explain them to me. They looked the same, except...I didn't understand why you'd have two almost identical sets. I guess I'll eventually learn. I made very high marks in school and learned very fast."

The man's smile faltered for a second. "I'm sure you did, Minnie. You keep working hard like you do, and soon you'll be running the restaurant for me."

"Oh my, I never dreamed I'd ever be the boss of anything," Minnie smiled wide.

Then the gentleman excused himself and left. The two ladies talked for a moment longer, and then Alice excused herself to. Minnie ordered her bread and sweet cakes, and headed home.

CHAPTER 24

Minnie had been surprised when she was given the position of Restaurant Manager. After the owner left that day, he'd gone straight to the old Manager, and confronted her about copying the books. It didn't take long for him to get a confession, and when Minnie came into work the next day, the woman was already gone.

As Minnie looked over the crowed dining room, inspecting the servers as they waited on customers, she knew she had no choice but to do her best, and continue to put her customers first.

Minnie walked to random tables, asking diners if everything was okay, and if there was anything she could do for them. Occasionally, she would wave or speak to her regular customers. Some of them were in so often, Minnie felt that she was their friend. She could tell you almost everything about their children and sometimes. Because of the unwanted information given to her, she could tell you about their household staff, and the woes of having servants. She would just smile and shake her head, and be sympathetic like she knew what it was to have household staff.

Walking back to her office, she noticed the calendar on the wall beside her door. Could this be right? She'd lived in Dallas for almost three years now.

The effects of the Great Depression were receding in Dallas. The economy was picking up. Once again, petroleum companies were starting to hire. It was slow, but steady. There was a push by the government to pave more roads across the country, and there were several dams being built to aid in the increased need for electricity as cities started to grow. As the financial outlook began to correct itself, trickles of news about America's possible involvement in the political unrest in Germany and France began to circulate.

Minnie had made a few friends, but she let work consume her. She could not seem to form lasting friendships here like she had in Tennessee. Maybe it was because when you're in your birth place, everyone gets you. You think the same way about things. Some may be better off financially, but the way you lived and worked were similar. Here in Dallas, everyone seemed to walk around like they were the very one that struck the oil. Yes, all benefited, but she saw no difference in her and the people she worked with.

Still, Minnie often had to repeat herself, or interpret a word or phrase so people understood what she was saying. Her accent had not changed much. But as a whole though, the people of Dallas were very hospitable.

She spent her spare time at the movie house.

Grace Moore was making more and more movies. Minnie never missed one, and sometimes would watch them a second time. She was out in the dining room before opening, when a beautiful lady unhooked the velvet rope, re-hooked it, and started toward her. They recognized each other at the same time. It was Grace Moore.

"Minnie Leigh, is that you? Didn't I leave you in Knoxville?" she beamed with joy.

"Well, I left you packing for France," Minnie laughed.

"It *is* you! What on earth are you doing in Dallas, Texas?"

Minnie shrugged and smiled. "Just decided to pack up and head out here. There was talk of businesses closing down, banks taking our money, and closing shop. I grabbed all of mine, bought a train ticket, and headed this way. What're you doing in Texas, Grace?"

"I'm promoting my new movie, posing for pictures and giving interviews for papers and magazines," she smiled.

"That's exciting! I go to the movie house and watch your movie's every chance I get. It's not as often now that I manage the restaurant. Come sit, I'll get us some coffee. Do you have time to talk?"

"Sure, I came in to see if I could get a small breakfast."

"What would you like? I'll have the cook whip you something up. I'm the Manager, you know," Minnie explained with great pride.

After taking Grace's order, Minnie entered the kitchen, gave the cook the order, fixed two cups of coffee, and returned to talk with her friend.

"Manager!" Grace repeated. "Congratulations Minnie, you've come a long way since we met. You look different, strong, more confident. Look at us two mountain girls setting the world on fire."

"I'm not like you, Grace," Minnie smiled softly. "You're a movie star. You can go anywhere in the world, and everyone knows who you are. I just run a restaurant, but I do love what I do. I enjoy meeting people from all over the country."

Grace looked off a bit. "There's a lot left to be desired as an actress and singer, Minnie. It's glamorous, and I never want for anything. But sometimes it would be nice to have the peace of the mountains of Tennessee." She looked back at Minnie. "That may change soon too. I heard that they are going to take the land from many families, name the mountains, and make it a National Park."

The cook came through the doors, placing a plate of food in front of Grace, and then freshened their coffee. He asked if they needed anything else before returning to the kitchen to complete his preparations for the day.

"I've read something about it," Minnie frowned. "I don't understand why they'd have to take the land from anyone. Some of those families have been there since Daniel Boone first hunted and trapped the land before it was ever a state. Well, not them, but their families. It's rightfully their land. It's good that they want to protect the land and mountains that it can never can be owned by one person, but to take their homes? I just don't know."

"It'll be done in phases," Grace explained. "The area where we come from isn't included in the original plan. Most families are cutting timber, most of them never knew they could sell the timber off. Logging companies would come in and pay them a fee, and sell the timber for four times as much. It's a big business now that the country is on the upswing. There's the talk of America joining forces if Europe goes to war."

"I hope that war doesn't come over here," Minnie shook her head. "It's bad enough that our men will once again go to a foreign land to help protect their families. But if I understand it right, the reason for sending soldiers over there is so the war will not come to America."

"That's what they say, Minnie," Grace nodded, then changed the subject. "Tell me now, have you married? Children? What else is going on with you beside running this restaurant?"

"No, I'm not married. I've gone to a dance or two with a couple of fellas I've met in here. I go to the zoo a lot, I love walking through seeing the different animals. It makes me dream of what rest of the world must be like. I don't want to travel, I don't know that I'd like the ocean liners. And more and more people are flying in those airplanes. Just doesn't seem natural."

Grace laughed. "It's so exciting to see and discover new places Minnie. But as I said sometimes, I get tired of traveling. It's what I chose to do, and it does give me the freedom to live anywhere and anyway I choose. You have to learn to be good to yourself."

She finished her meal. Opening time was fast approaching. The ladies hugged, promised to stay in touch, and said their goodbyes.

After work, Minnie decided to do as Grace suggested, to be kind to herself.

Minnie Leigh was not one to shop as other women did. She never could understand how clothes or having more than one could make anyone happy.

Neiman-Marcus was introducing a new line of clothing, and it was the buzz about town. Minnie decided for once, she would see what the fuss was about. She'd never visited the *Sanger Department Stores*, or *Neiman-Marcus*. They were a source of pride for Dallas. *Neiman-Marcus* was one of the leading fashions outlets in the country, and one of the owners and designers of their clothing was known worldwide.

She didn't know what to expect when she arrived. She did enjoy walking past their window displays, which had become as famous as the store itself. She often heard locals, as well as visitors, remark that they didn't want to forget to visit *Neiman-Marcus* because they had a new window display. They were artistic and innovative.

Walking on the opposite side of the street, Minnie stopped as she arrived in front of the *Neiman-Marcus* building. There they were, the grand windows, but even standing back this distance, you couldn't see the full display. The crowds around the window blocked her view.

Minnie crossed the street and walked into the store. As she entered the store, she couldn't believe her eyes. The very ceiling looked like it never ended. Everything sparkled like diamonds and jewels. There were counters filled with bottled perfumes from across the world, and other display counters were filled with jewelry.

At a leisurely pace, Minnie moved through the store until she found the area filled with racks and racks of women's clothing, the latest styles in every fabric and every color one could imagine. But Minnie didn't stop to look through the dresses as she was curious about the floor above her.

She walked to the elevator, another first, and took it to the next level. As she stepped off the elevator, she moved to the rail that allowed her to look down on the main floor. From this vantage point, she could see everything, and what a grand sight it was.

Minnie explored the other levels like men's wear and shoes for men and women. There was one floor that was lady's lingerie. Until now, Minnie had never seen such fine undergarments. and had never imagined some of them existed. The last level she visited contained furniture, all arranged in matching sets to assist customers in visualizing what it would look like in their own homes.

Minnie had bought nothing, but had one of the best days ever. She never realized that there could be such a grand place. She now started to see how people could be caught up in the beauty and grandness of it all. One had to control themselves really. Minnie herself had felt the draw, and almost needed to have one of everything. A lesser controlled person could spend money they didn't have to try to impress others of their good taste.

Walking out of the store and toward her apartment, Minnie felt intoxicated by all the finery.

CHAPTER 25

The months passed, one after the other, without much change. Business and crowds at the restaurant followed the economic flow.

Minnie spent her spare time exploring the city. She'd also found Dallas had one of the most extensive public libraries. She enjoyed going through the racks of books and choosing just one. Then walking to the park, she'd look until she found the perfect tree to lean against, sit, and read her book until the sun began setting. Shopping never did take hold of her though, but she did add to her wardrobe. She kept it minimal.

Dallas provided plenty of entertainment. From time to time, she would accept the invitation of a gentleman, but never felt interested in staying with one gentleman more than any other.

Another year passed. It was now 1934, and there was political news of something called the Texas Centennial Exposition. Dallas, Houston, and San Antonio would compete to host the celebration. They all vied for the honor, as well as the economic boost. This would be the largest and most elaborate celebration of the anniversary of Texas's independence from Mexico. The festival would not take place until 1936, but there were plans to be made and money to raise. Many felt the campaign would be a long hard-fought battle between the three cities.

The restaurant afforded Minnie the pleasure of meeting new and up-and-coming entertainers. Sometimes entertainers that had already made it would take rooms at the hotel. She always took care to treat them well, and thank them for their patronage. She made sure all the customers felt appreciated. Occasionally, there would be an entertainer that would demand more attention, all the while saying not to fuss over them. She was sure they wanted everyone to notice them.

Magazines like "Photoplay," "Screenland," and "Modern Screen" had become a habit. She was elated to spot Grace Moore on the cover of both "Screenplay" and "Photoplay."

Just think, I call her my friend, Minnie would think. Both articles hailed her performance in her last film, and were raving about her ability to maintain her pace between making movies and performing opera.

Minnie used such articles as a means of keeping up with her friend during their dry spells of actual visits. She also found she enjoyed reading about the lives of other famous people. Advertisements were calling for *"Fresh New Faces,"* and *"Fresh New Talent."*

As Minnie read the bios on various stars. She realized they were everyday people, and many came from simple, hard-working families. Occasionally, she would entertain the idea of becoming a star herself. If Grace, a girl from the same mountain she came from, could make it big, why couldn't she? But he would just put it out of her head because all the gallantry and finery that came along with stardom frightened her. She couldn't see herself posing for the press or dressing in fancy clothes just to go out to lunch or a night on the town.

Never the less, she began to read books about California and how Los Angeles was building up and developing into a city centered around the *rich and famous*.

She found out that Los Angeles had been the center of many conflicts surrounding migrant workers and displaced families caused by the Great Depression and labor unions. California farmers had taken full advantage of people hit hard by the depression. Those less fortunate came by the droves looking for work. They prayed for a means of providing for their families, and dreamed for a better life.

Minnie learned that many people were dying from starvation and diseases brought on by weakened immune systems. The old and very young were stricken. Cheap labor meant more profit for growers. Shanty towns sprung up in those areas, as those still looking to recover from the effects of the depression sought work. Once there, many found out that the pay was minimal and seasonal. The regular annual pickers were being put out of work for the cheap labor that starving families provided. This caused an increase in violence.

After reading article after article and book after book, she began to think of moving out to California. But would it be in her best interest? Minnie had moved to Dallas during a population growth. The construction seemed endless, and though the excitement of watching history in the making was an indescribable feeling, she wasn't sure that she wanted to live through it again. She would have to put much prayer and thought into another big move.

Entering the park, which had become her evening ritual, she found a quiet spot well off the typical path.

"God, it's Minnie Leigh. Just needed to talk for a while. I have so much on my mind, and I don't know which way to turn. I have a job that I like, and Dallas has been good to me. I have and am learning so many things. No matter where I am, you seem to surround me with the most exciting people. I've met the lowest, the hungriest, the famous, and some of the richest. I find that most are no different from the rest of us. They all want someone to hear their heart. There've been a few that would hide everything about themselves. Most I see as hurting, but some are evil and deceptive.

"Even with all the blessings, I find my own heart is torn again with where I should be or where I should go. My friend Grace, she's from my mountain. She's a great movie star and sings like a bird.
I read in the movie magazines of the grand life she and others lead. It seems like a dream. I'm curious what California is like. Why do all these people from all walks of life go to California?

Is it for a better life? Do they like to pretend so much that they must act? They make a lot of money for play acting while others starve. Is that ok? I think I could do that. The only thing is, I can't see keeping all that money when so many are hungry and without homes. What should I do? Do I move again? Do I stay here? I, as always, will wait for your answer. You haven't led me wrong this far."

Minnie sat for a while longer in the quiet, waiting. Waiting for what? She did not know. The more she talked to God, the more she expected to hear Him speak to her. After a while, she stood to head home. She gave a glance toward heaven. "Well, I'll be going, and I thank you for listening."

Tonight, she didn't read, or look to be entertained. She sat quietly on her couch and waited, lost in thought and trying to decide what she wanted for the rest of her life.

CHAPTER 26

Minnie's life continued much as always. Working, going out with friends, and frequent visits to the library. She added volunteering to her long list of activities. She loved to work soup lines and assisting displaced families. When she could, she would direct them to part-time jobs, hiring some herself to work in the restaurant. However, the unrest in her over a move to California remained. As a result, she sought out more and more things to occupy her mind.

Participating in the campaign for Dallas to host the Texas Independence Exhibit became a real joy for her. Texans understandably were divided, mostly between choosing San Antonio and Dallas as the host city. The Alamo in San Antonio was the site where the original fight began, and so many brave Americans, Mexicans, and Native Americans fought for the United States' independence from Mexico, and the tyranny of Santa Ana.

For Minnie, Dallas, the place she now called home, found favor as she had witnessed the success of Dallas resources in protecting its citizens from the effects of the Great Depression. She was full of pride and excitement when everyone's efforts were realized upon the announcement that Dallas would be the official host city of the upcoming celebration. To outbid and out plan Houston and San Antonio was quite a feat.

Now that this battle had been won, the politicians, architects, and planners would begin construction on the site for the celebration. The project would combine nostalgia from the state's romantic past with a desire to address a hopeful future.

Architects such as Wyatt Hedrick, Donald Nelson, and Elmer Withers created timeless tableaus of Texas history. More than fifty buildings would be built, and jobs were always welcome by the citizens looking to improve their lives and reach for long-sought dreams.

The one-hundred-year anniversary would be held at *State Fair Park*. The landscaped expanse would encompass one hundred and seventy-eight acres of prime property.

New activity in town spread enthusiasm and an overall feeling of wellbeing. Every business in the city made plans to be a part of the upcoming celebration. Though two years away, many felt early planning would reap the most significant rewards.

The Adolphus Hotel was no exception. Plans were made to remodel the rooms and spruce up the lobby. New China, fresh paint, and new wall hangings were ordered for the restaurant.

Minnie was planning to hire additional servers to handle the expected visitors. She wanted to be a little ahead of the celebration. This would allow the servers to be well trained and professional by the time the exhibit opened in June of 1936. The remodel, however, would be her foremost project.

The dining room would have to be rearranged to accommodate construction workers and painters. Hopefully, most of the work could be done during the hours they were closed. She was proud of the profit her little restaurant made, and didn't want it interrupted.

The temperatures in the fall in east Texas continued to be quite hot. The cool down didn't arrive until November that year. Usually the rain came this time of year. However, the showers had been very few and far between across the country.

The dust from the Midwest was reported to black out Amarillo for fifteen hours. There were a few days in Dallas that dust seemed to seep through walls. Minnie and the servers work tirelessly wiping and cleaning everything. Water pitchers had to continually be washed and refilled to assure customers had dust-free water. Dinner plates had to be covered from the kitchen to the dining room until placed in front of the patrons. All windows and doors, including the hotel lobby doors which were typically left open, were kept closed to help combat the problem. A doorman was stationed to assure the doors were never left open.

Even though the *Adolphus* was among the most modern of buildings with indoor air, the overwhelmingly stuffy, dry air made Minnie and her staff miserable. Minnie felt unusual exhaustion at the end of the day, so her trips to the library and park were waylaid as the need and desire to soak in a tub of fresh water seemed more inviting. Her evenings were spent idle, re-reading magazines and books she owned.

When the break finally came, the rain was tremendous. The new levees along the Trinity River completed mid-town and downtown Dallas were spared from flooding. The city was saved, but the levees caused an overflow downstream. Farmland was flooded, and families were displaced.

After work, Minnie threw herself into assisting with clean up in flooded areas. She started a drive for clothes and food for flood victims, asking her more affluent customers for assistance. By Christmas, repair and reconstruction of flood victim's homes were well underway, and Christmas packages for their children containing everything from toys to clothing were distributed. In preparation for the Centennial Exhibit, Minnie began to refocus on the remodel as 1935 arrived.

Minnie Leigh more and more went through her days despondent. Work, volunteering and even her free time became taxing. Everything she did made her tired. She was losing her desire, her drive to be involved in it all.

Minnie sat in her quiet place in the park.

"Dear God, I don't feel like I have a lot to say. I'm heavy inside."

Minnie sat quietly for a while, not knowing where to begin, not knowing what it was she was feeling. "God, how do I tell you what I feel when I don't understand it myself? There's been so much, starting way back; back when the dust was dry-ing my soul out, and the heat wouldn't let me breathe. Then instead of a gentle rain washing it away, you opened the heavens. I feel like I didn't do enough for those people. Some houses washed clean away. Others filled up with water. How do I help in times like that? I cooked and gathered clothes. When I could, I found jobs for the womenfolk. It still didn't feel like enough.

"And all the while I was running the restaurant and kept on going. I barely remember Christmas and the New Year's arrival. Every day just seems like the one before it. I was excited about the remodel, and the restaurant has fresh paint.

"I know I shouldn't be whining, I have more than I need. Really, nothing seems to fill the emptiness inside of me."

Walking home, Minnie spotted a new Movie poster plastered on the side of the Movie Theater. *"JENETTE MCDONALD AND EDDY NELSON in VICTOR HERBERTS "NAUGHTY MARIETTA.""*

It hailed Miss McDonald the most significant female singer ever! Minnie laughed and shook her head. "No one sings better than Grace Moore!" She found herself becoming angry about the movie poster.

She then stopped in at the A&P Grocery store. All the way through the store, while picking up items she needed, she mumbled to herself. "What is the world coming to? We buy our food in stores instead of growing it. Look at this!" she said out loud. "Can you believe ten pounds sugar is forty-nine cents, thirty cents a pound for bacon, and lard is a dollar and six cents for one carton? How are regular people supposed to live? You spend all your money just tryin' to eat to survive."

The grocery manager walked over and gently touched Minnie on the shoulder. Until then, she wasn't aware that customers had stopped to stare. Embarrassed, she set her basket down and left the store.

Walking, almost running to her apartment, she could barely contain herself. Quickly slamming the door behind her, she slid to the floor and began crying. She couldn't believe she had lost her senses in public.

"What is *wrong* with me? God, *help me!*" Standing and pacing back and forth, Minnie tried to figure out where the heaviness was coming from. Why was she feeling so angry? She had no one to be mad at, for any reason. She had everything she needed and more. She filled the tub with hot water and climbed in and tried to relax.

As her muscles began to soften, she found herself crying. Crying was not something she often did, but this time, she let her tears flow. When she was exhausted from crying, and the water was cold, she climbed out of the tub and put her house-coat on. She was nearly asleep before she laid on her bed.

Minnie woke sometime during the night and crawled under her covers. She had one thought as sleep overtook her once more: being alone, with no one to share life with, she was very lonely.

When she woke the next morning and slowly prepared for work, she remembered her last thought as she had fallen back to sleep. The heaviness returned. As it did, she also felt angry with herself for being weak. As she walked to work, she thought more about her circumstances, and decided she would do something about it.

During lunch, she saw one of her gentlemen friends. Walking over to the table, she greeted him with a more prominent smile than was usual. "So, Joe what's going on in town tonight? I feel like getting out for a while, would you mind escorting me?"

Taking a deep breath and trying not to seem too excited, Joe sat up straight. "*The Majestic* had Bing Crosby a couple of weeks ago. We could walk over there and see who is playing tonight. Or we could catch a picture show."

"I was thinking more of dancing and music. I've not been dancing in a while."

"Oh, okay. Well, I'll find the best place," he smiled.

"Sure Joe, I'll be ready around...um, what time you're picking me up?"

"How's six? Is that too late?"

"Well no, I hear the music doesn't get swinging until

seven or eight."

After making plans, Minnie went back to her office and killed time completing her paperwork and ordering supplies for the restaurant. She would take short breaks and walk thru the dining area, smiling and nodding her head, not wanting to talk to anyone today.

CHAPTER 27

Minnie was dressed in a white dress with green accents. She'd bought a matching green wrap. One last check to make sure the seams of her stockings were straight before putting on her white heels, she took one a look in the mirror to check that her hair was in place. She'd followed the advice found in the fashion magazines, and was wearing her makeup a little heavier for her night out with Joe. It had taken her a little while to get it on just right, but she was pleased with the results.

As she was making her inspection, there was a knock on the door. Minnie shrugged her shoulders, and gave herself a slight smile before opening the door to find Joe dressed in a navy pinstripe suit holding his Fedora in his hands. *A true gentleman, and he cleans up well*, she thought to herself.

"Hey-ya, Minnie," he smiled wide.

"Hey-ya, Joe. Shall we go?"

"Yes, yes, by all means," Joe replied.

Walking a few feet out from Minnie, Joe was inspecting his date with a broad smile on his face.

"What you are looking at, Joe?" Minnie asked as crooked smile crossed her lips.

"You're looking really nice tonight, Minnie," his smile widened.

"Thank you, Joe. Do I look so awful at the diner?" she joked.

"No Minnie, but you look extra special tonight. Did you decide where you want to go?"

"Anywhere the music is hopping, and I can get a drink,"

Minnie shrugged.

"Drink? Drink as in alcoholic beverage?" Joe was dumb founded. He always believed Minnie Leigh to be a lady of the highest standard. Now he wondered.

Joe had wanted to court Minnie for the longest, but it was always two dates, then nothing. The time span between dates this time had been about four months. However, she'd been volunteering with flood victims in November, and pre-occupied with the restaurant remodel these last two months. At least that's what she had told him.

It didn't matter, tonight she was his sweetheart.

They caught a Trolley to the edge of town. They jumped off, hand in hand, as it slowed in the curve that would start it back on track toward the town center.

"So where're we going, Joe?"

"I asked around and I was told the place for music and dancing would be the *Texas Tavern*. If we want to listen to blues, we have to go down on Central to *The Gypsy Tea Room*. However, I hear *The Tea Room* can get really rough."

"Sounds like just what the Doctor ordered," Minnie said.

Joe raised an eyebrow. "Minnie, are you sure this's what you want to do? I can take you to one of the nicer dinner clubs, with musical acts and dancing."

"No, Joe." Taking him by the elbow, she flashed a teasing smile. Minnie had plans Joe knew nothing about. She knew this afternoon that she was out to dance and drink and *to hell* with everything else. She was tired of feeling so down. The only way she knew to chase the blues away was to throw a hoe down.

Since moving to Dallas, she hadn't ventured anywhere near the taverns and tea rooms. Her mood had become so heavy, she felt that the only thing to do was to loosen it up a bit.

As they entered the Texas Tavern, The Boswell Sisters were on stage. Minnie had heard that they had stopped touring and couldn't believe her eyes. They were singing "That's How the Rhythm Born," and right away, Minnie felt her spirit lift. The sound of the banjo playing reminded her of home.

Excitedly, she threw her bag and shawl on a table and grabbed Joe's hand and pulled him to the dance floor.

Joe moaned and protested that he couldn't dance, but Minnie didn't hear him, or didn't care to. She could only feel the rhythm of the music.

After dancing through a few songs, she abruptly walked back to the table, gathered her things, and moved over to the bar with little thought to what Joe may think. She was in a trance, feeling her mountain roots drive her every move.

"Minnie," Joe said. "Why don't we get a table? Or at least let me order your drink. It's not very lady-like for you to order liquor."

Minnie laughed, but backed off and let Joe walk up to the bar in her place. He'd taken on more than he knew.

Although she was a few years younger than Joe, she seemed to have more life experience. Joe had been raised in a family where he was protected. He knew all the social rules and lived by them. Minnie, on the other hand, was one to learn as she went. Before Betty had taken her in, she'd had no one to turn to for advice about anything, much less behavior and manners. Tonight, she knew that her choices would break at least some of the social rules, but she didn't care. She'd planned to drink as much as she wanted, and dance until she could dance no more.

Drinking down three shots of whiskey, and a few sips of Joe's beer, she took him by the arm. She was hankering to hit the dance floor. She did pause to think of appearances as she politely and steadily guided him back to the floor.

This time, the music was slower and more to Joe's liking. They hadn't spoken a word to one another since they had walked up to the bar. Joe was feeling a little uncomfortable, and until Minnie wrapped her arms around his neck, a little put-out. They danced two slow dances, and then Joe took her by the hand, went to the bar, gathered her belongings, found them a table, and sat down.

"Minnie, are you ok? You're acting like, like ..."

"Like what Joe?"

"I'm not sure, Minnie," he sighed. "We've been out before, and I never thought you would take a drink. Here you are, drinking like a man. One minute you're dancing like a savage, and the next minute, you have your arms around my neck, gliding across the dance floor like a soft breeze. Are you okay?"

Minnie just shrugged. "Joe, I don't know how to explain it. I feel like dancing and drinking tonight. I've been feeling out of sorts lately, and the only way I know to right it is to have a hoe down. Now, no one here seems to know what I mean, so the only thing I know to do is get where there's music and liquor and have a good time. It's the way I was raised up, and I know no other way."

Joe was a gentle sort of guy, the hero type. He took Minnie confiding in him as a sign that she wanted him to be her guy, and as he had watched his father do, he would help Minnie get past what she was going through. With that thought, he walked back to the bar, and ordered two more whiskies and a beer. He and Minnie stayed at the Texas Room drinking and dancing until they both had difficulty moving without stumbling.

With a drunken smile, Minnie asked, "What you say Joe? We get out of here?"

With slurred speech and a smile, he said, "You know, I was just thinking the same thing."

He helped her with her wrap the best he could, and she looped her arm through his. They moved with unsteady gaits toward the door.

"We'll have to walk a few blocks. The streetcars don't run here this time of night or morning. Whatever it is."

"Good," said Minnie "I feel like walking a spell."

Then Joe laughed. "Your voice sounds funny, Minnie."

Stopping, she looked at him with fire in her eyes. "Funny? What do you'ins mean *funny*?"

"*You'ins*. What on earth kind of language is that?"

"*You'ins, you, ya'll*; whatever it is you'ins use in this crazy place. I shoulda never come here," she frowned. "No one makes sense. You'ins shop and spend money every day like it's nothing in this town. Look how big it is! Who needs all these buildings? They just keep building them higher and higher. Where they tryin' to get? Heaven?"

"I don't know where you were born Minnie, but I've never heard anyone with such an accent. You sound like some hick. And what's wrong with Dallas wanting to be the biggest and the best?"

"*I am not a hick!*" Minnie snapped. "I am a *HILLBIILLY* from *TENNESEE!*" Minnie shouted with her drunken pride. "And what's the use in blocking out the sun? No wonder everyone has to go to a store to buy vegetables. There's no sun! Look around; no one lives in a real house. They live in apartments and apartment buildings. Where your chilen's going to go to dig their toes in the dirt? Or climb a tree? The sun and the moon are completely up in the sky by the times anyone can see'em. How's ya going to greet the day properly?"

"Minnie, what are you going on about? You're not making any sense," Joe shook his head, his face showing his confusion.

Eight blocks later, they were nearly to the center of town. Joe steered Minnie toward one of the all-night cafés, sat her down, and insisted she order something to eat. As they both started sobering up, Minnie began to feel embarrassed by her behavior.

"I'm sorry, Joe, for the way I've acted tonight. I don't know what's going on with me," she sighed.

"Minnie, I believe what you need is a husband," he started. "A good husband. One that can be an ear when you need it, one that comforts you when you feel down, one that can share your joy and heart aches. If you would allow me, I'd like to court you with the intentions of being your husband. I could take good care of you. You could quit working, and we could get a nice apartment close to the park. I know that you like to take long walks there. I've seen you from time to time just sitting there in the grass, taking in the sun. In those moments, you're as pretty as a picture to me, and I think I could make you a good husband. One you would be proud of."

"No. No, Joe," Minnie shook her head. "I don't want a husband. Why on earth would I want to live in an apartment forever?"

"I'm not saying an apartment as you live in now, Minnie. I'm talking about one like my parents raised us in, two or three stories. There would be plenty of room for children and dinner parties—"

Minnie held up her hand. "Stop right there. I don't know what I've ever said or done that would lead you to believe I want or need a husband, Joe."

"Maybe you haven't. I just felt like you're sharing such intimate feelings earlier, you were letting me know you needed a husband. Minnie, I want to be that husband," he tried to smile.

Getting up quickly, throwing her wrap around her shoulders and grabbing her purse, Minnie ran out of the café. Had she said something or done something that made this man think that she needed him?

"What am I doing? I've lost my mind! I asked him out. I let him pay for my drinks and food. How crazy can I be?! Of *course*, he thinks I'm his girl! Why didn't I pay my way?" Her mind was shooting questions a mile a minute. She couldn't keep up with her thoughts.

As she made her way into her apartment, she could no longer hold back the tears. She had no idea what was going on. Was she losing her mind?

Minnie tried to calm herself by splashing cold water on her face. She had to stop again and again to catch her breath. She wasn't just crying tonight, she was sobbing.

"I'm so lonely, God help me! What am I supposed to do? I'm social with others, but my only friends are far off in Bean Station. I do things to help people out when I see they have a need, but still I feel unfulfilled. All these years, and not one word from any of my brothers, or my Paw. What did I do? Why am I nothing to them? Why have I been thrown away?"

Sleep overtook her as her thoughts continued to race through her head. The awful, lonely feelings were now coupled with the guilt of giving Joe the wrong impression. Not once did she stop to think about the implications Joe would get from her asking him to take her out dancing, letting him buy her drinks, and being there to watch out for her when she followed through on her intent to get drunk to shake all these negative feelings coursing through her vein of late. She was guilty, guilty of allowing her own selfish needs to impact the heart of another person. Not just any person. A friend.

The next morning, Minnie woke up to find the sun full in the sky and her head pounding. She jumped to her feet. The clock said ten AM.

"What on earth! I've never slept past the sun rising!"

Running into the bathroom, she dressed, combed, and pulled her hair up in a quick do. She hastily slipped on her shoes, ran out of her apartment, and down the street toward the restaurant.

When she arrived, everything seemed reasonable. As she passed through the dining room, she nodded to the patrons, and spoke a greeting to her regulars. She made her way to the kitchen where she gave the head cook a nod. As she entered her office, she shut the door behind her.

Minnie busied herself with counting and balancing the cash from the safe with the receipts from the previous day, just as she did every day. Once the deposit was ready, she gathered the bag, and headed out to the bank.

As she walked down the street to the bank, she was stopped several times by various people asking her to volunteer for one charity or another. Minnie Leigh told all of them she would think about it. Lost in her thoughts, she began counting the years she'd been away from her mountain. It had been nine years. She was now twenty-two years old, and still without children or a proper home.

As the heat of summer came boiling in, the construction finally started on the hotel. It had been decided that the remodel of the restaurant would be held until the end of the year, or just after the new year.

The preparations for the Centennial Exhibition intensified, and allowed Minnie to push the loneliness away. The excitement and extra work consumed her. The owners of the Adolphus Hotel and restaurant seemed to raise expectations on a weekly basis. Minnie was determined to meet every one of them. A record number of visitors, celebrities, and dignitaries were expected to move into the city for the much-anticipated celebration. There was even talk of President Roosevelt himself attending. Imagine, the most powerful person in this whole big country visiting Dallas, Texas.

Working together with her head cook, Minnie developed a new menu. She researched diligently to find the best recipes. She felt useful. She came in early and left late. The work was good for the mood that had consumed her for far too long.

She wrote Miss Betty regularly, but very rarely heard back. It had been a while since she had heard from anyone from Bean Station. She had sent a telegraph several weeks ago inviting Miss Betty and Sadie to Texas for the celebration, hoping, but not expecting, either to show.

"Miss Minnie, will you please come to the lobby?" she heard over a speaker. It was strange hearing such a thing, like God speaking to you from heaven. You could hear it, but no one was in sight.

Arriving at the desk, she was handed the phone. This was another first for Minnie. She had been around phones, but she had never used one. She held it to her ear, as she had seen others do. When she finally said "Hello?" she heard Sadie saying *"Hello? Hello? Minnie, are you there?"*

"Oh, my goodness, Sadie? Sadie, is that you?"

"Minnie, can you hear me ok?"

"Yes, I hear you fine! I've never talked on a phone before. Oh my goodness, is that you?"

"Yes, Miss Betty put a phone in the café!" Sadie explained. "Everyone wants to say hello. Hold on."

There was some shuffling. "Minnie? Minnie, it's Lilly Mae and Big Joe. Can you hear me, child?"

"Yes, Lilly, I can hear you," she smiled. "Tell Big Joe hello!"

"He can hear you! Tell him yourself."

"Hey Big Joe, are you keeping Lilly Mae out of trouble?"

"Child, you talkin' bout real work there. Big Joe is takin' it easy these days," Big Joe laughed.

"Don't listen to him a, child. When are you comin' back home?"

"Not for a while, Lilly. I'm the manager of a big restaurant here in Dallas."

"Well come home when you can!"

There was more shuffling. "Minnie? Minnie, this is Miss Betty."

Hearing Miss Betty's voice brought tears to Minnie's eyes. The lump in her throat swelled 'til she could hardly speak. "Hey, Miss Betty. How are you? I can't believe we're talking on a phone!"

"Me either, child. I never thought I'd have a phone in my café."

"I'm so glad you do," Minnie sniffled a bit. "I've been so homesick for all of you." The tears began to flow.

"Minnie, are you okay?"

"Yes, Miss Betty. I am now. Are you and Sadie going to come out to Texas for the big celebration?"

"No, Minnie. I'm sorry, we can't," Miss Betty said. "I'll let Sadie tell you. I love you, girl. You come home as soon as you can."

"I love you too, Miss Betty."

Shuffling again, "Minnie, Minnie, it's Sadie again."

"Yes, Sadie. Why can't you and Miss Betty come to Texas? It takes just a week by train. You can stay a week or two and then go back. We would have a great time! Dallas is a much nicer city than Knoxville," Minnie tried to persuade her friend.

"Minnie, we can't come because I'm expecting. Doc said it would not be good for me to travel that far because I'll be too close to the baby's due date."

Minnie held her breath. She could not believe what she

was hearing. She 'd been gone a long time, but now that she was speaking to her friend, it didn't seem like any time at all.

"Minnie, did you hear me?" Sadie asked. "I'm going to have a baby!"

"I heard you! Oh, Sadie that's so exciting! I wish I was there with you," Minnie smiled softly.

"I wish you were too. If it's a girl, I'm going to call her Leigh after you. You're my best friend, after all. Her first name will be Anna, after my Maw, even though I never knew her well."

"Anna Leigh. That's a real nice name Sadie."

"We have to say good bye now, Minnie. Take care of yourself. Sorry I haven't written you more, I'll try to do better. I love you, my friend."

"I love you too, Sadie. Give Miss Betty a hug and kiss for me. Tell everyone I said hello."

With that, the call was disconnected. Even though Minnie was sad to have to hang up, she felt like a new person. All the despair she had felt over the last few weeks just melted away. She knew she was loved and missed.

As she walked back to her office, she realized that her prayer had been answered. For the first time, she was aware of a concrete answer to a direct prayer to God. As she sat at her desk, she was overcome with a sense of wellbeing. She just realized that in all her years of talking to God, He had to be real. No way could it just be by chance that Miss Betty had picked the very moment she needed her so bad to have a phone installed in her café.

CHAPTER 28

The first of the year 1936 came without much to do for Minnie. Every day, she played and replayed her conversation with her friends in Bean Station. She'd asked about using the phone at the desk several times, but after getting the price of the call, she knew she couldn't afford it.

She kept herself busy as planned. She never saw Joe in the restaurant again. She heard that he'd moved north to help his father and learn how to manage the oil wells. He would soon take over his father's position. She hoped the best for him, and wanted to know he was happy. She didn't blame him for never speaking to her again after the grave way she acted when he openly expressed his feelings and proposed marriage.

May rolled around, and the remodeling crew moved into the dining room. Even though Minnie went to a lot of trouble to re-arrange the tables to accommodate, the crowd fell off considerably. As soon as the construction was over, Minnie asked for a group of volunteers to work late into the night to clean tables and wipe down everything in the dining room. In the kitchen, the head cook and two others scrubbed every surface and floor until you could've eaten off them. Once the job was complete, she expressed her gratitude for everyone's help.

Minnie then set about placing the new table clothes and setting the China just so. She measured the cups and silverware as she had seen in the books she'd studied over the last year. She turned out the lights, not looking back as she closed the door. She wanted to arrive early the next morning, and see everything with fresh eyes.

Minnie woke earlier than usual, and enjoyed her coffee and breakfast at home before heading out to the restaurant. As she unlocked the doors and switched on the lights, she couldn't believe her eyes. The room was gleaming. She felt a new sense of fulfillment. Her hard work had paid off, but she recognized the contributions of many in helping her to reach this day.

June came, and the Exhibition started. The crowds were overwhelming. Minnie labored tirelessly to ensure the food was perfect, and the service top grade.

In the middle of a hectic rush, Minnie was approached by a delivery boy who held in his hand an urgent telegram. Minnie's stomach sank.

The only urgent telegrams she had ever heard of were notifications of death. Signing for the telegram, she was fearful of what it would tell her. Taking it in her hands, she slowly opened it, read it, and let a big smile cross her face.

"It's a girl!" Several of the customers looked up and smiled. "Sorry," she said. "It's my best friend, she had a little girl. She named her after me. I have a name sake."

Minnie had never felt more satisfied and a part of something as she felt right now. She was walking on air these days, and could ask for nothing else. Life was good for her. However, she kept pride at bay, and let gratitude fill her heart.

The three-month exhibition ended, and the crowds began to reduce, but only ever so slightly. Dallas, like always, continued to grow. The exhibition had enabled the shops and restaurants downtown to once again boom. Dallas and her citizens delivered on their exhibition campaign promises of boosting city commerce, and raising the national awareness of all the city has to offer.

CHAPTER 29

The remainder of the year passed, and with it, Minnie's loneliness grew. She had continued to pray and share her every thought and need to God.

As she did, there was the feeling that her time in Dallas had come to an end. This move would be different. She would take time to plan everything out. Her first instinct was to pack and move back to the mountains she missed so much. She had no desire to live anywhere else. There was, however, one more place she wanted to see: California.

Grace had spoken about it like a dream. It had to be a magic place. How else could they make the beautiful movies everyone enjoyed at all the movie houses?

Minnie Leigh continued to work. She frequented the library, looking up the history of California, concentrating on Los Angeles and anything else she could find that would help her with her plan to visit the west coast. The more she read the movie magazines and history of the area, the more she believed it to be a magical place.

It wasn't long before the visit to California turned into a move to California. Minnie became excited, and felt alive again as she prepared for the move.

Her ticket was bought, her clothes packed. She spent her last day in Dallas making sure she was square with everyone that she might have owed on a line of credit. The restaurant books were up to date, and the new manager was trained. Minnie Leigh had chosen a replacement from her staff that she knew could handle the job. The server had been with the restaurant longer than Minnie, and would do an excellent job.

Two weeks later, she was on a train heading west. She had a curiosity about Hollywood in California, and knew she must satisfy it before considering going back to her mountain home. Once she allowed herself to return, she'd never want to leave again.

She arrived in Los Angeles the following week, and much like before, she set out straight away to find an apartment and a job.

The La Belle was the third building Minnie visited. The landlord took one look at her, and shook his head. He told Minnie that one in fifty girls made it into pictures, and out of the fifty, maybe two made it in more than three films. Statistically, one out of that two would make as a mediocre star.

Minnie was too tired to explain to him she was not there to be in pictures. She had moved here more or less just to see what the fuss was all about. True to form, she quickly settled into a small apartment that suited her needs.

She continued, on her second day in town, looking for a job. All she could find right away was part-time counter help at the Dining Car.

She had saved her money wisely, which allowed her to take some time in finding a job she wanted. She would be careful with this plan, as she worried about another crash in the market. It was preparing ahead that kept her from falling into the same trap as others had during the depression.

Miss Betty had started her saving money from her daily tips for a *just in case* emergency. While in Dallas, Minnie had continued this saving regiment, but also added weekly from her salary. Minnie took her bank draft and deposited it in the nearest bank. When she was withdrawing her money from the bank in Dallas, she could not believe the amount.

Over her six-year stay in Dallas, she had saved eight-thousand dollars. She felt very rich.

Minnie was confused when the cashier handed her one piece of paper. She had brought with her a small carpet bag to put her money in for the trip. The cashier explained to her that the draft would allow her to travel in safety, and when she arrived at her destination, the bank of deposits would send for her money. Minnie was scared and relieved at the same time. She'd felt the weight of concern knowing she'd be traveling with all that money. Now, she was relieved that she had a bank draft.

She sent Grace Moore a telegram letting her know she was in Los Angeles, and if she came to town, to be sure to visit. It surprised her when she received a response telegram in which Grace let her know she didn't know when she would be in California, but she would visit when she did. She also told Minnie to speak to the owner of Frank's Grill, Frank Moretti, about a full-time position. Grace instructed her to let him know who sent her, and to be sure to share with him her references from Adolphus Hotel. Minnie inquired at Frank's Grill, as instructed, and within a few days, had a full-time job.

From time to time, she would notice a person or a group of very familiar looking people sitting together, but she couldn't place where she would know them from.

She went about her work and treated everyone with the same smile and service she had always provided. The original owners had sold the restaurant around 1927 from what she could gather, and she was told that the restaurant never did much business until the Moretti brothers took it over.

One day near the end of her shift, Mr. Moretti came to Minnie and asked her to help him take some trays of food and drinks to the back room. Minnie didn't understand why you'd take food and drink to a back room.

Hoisting the large tray on her shoulder, she then followed Mr. Moretti through the back hall and through a door she had not yet used. Minnie entered the room, and sat the tray down on an empty table, quickly realizing this was a whole other section of Frank's Grill.

It was known to its patrons as The Back Room. The room was used for celebrities and writers. Moretti got busy pouring drinks, and she would serve the plates after cleaning the table off.

Reaching to start gathering the papers scattered on the table, one of the gentlemen reached and gently grabbed her wrist. "We'll take care of the cleaning, sweetheart." She looked up with a smile to address Mr. Moretti.

Sweetheart. "Oh, my!" Minnie gasped, a little flattered.

"Yes, sweetheart. I'm me, and you're you. Now let's get this table cleaned off so you can serve us our lambchops."

"Yes, sir," Minnie blinked.

"Now gentleman, would you listen to that? *Yes, sir.* You guys should show me that kind of respect," he laughed.

Everyone else laughed including Minnie. She relaxed and served the plates. When it came time to leave the room, Minnie felt as if she was walking on a cloud. Moving here was the greatest thing she ever did. *Wait until Sadie and Miss Betty hear about this!*

Mr. Moretti thanked Minnie for staying to help, and slipped a five-dollar bill into her hand.

Walking the few blocks to her apartment in the warm balmy air of Los Angeles, she felt like a million bucks. And to make her steps even lighter, she had just met *Mr. Sweetheart* in person.

Minnie settled into Los Angeles and found every day an adventure. She never knew who she would meet at work, or whom she might bump into at the market.

Her employer had taught her how to protect the celebrity clientele against crazy fans that might slip in once in a while by using redirection tactics, careful to never make a scene. Minnie had never treated celebrities at Adolphus any different from a typical joe, and she wouldn't start now. Giving every patron the utmost respect secured their loyalty, and gained the business word of mouth advertisement. A win-win for everyone.

Minnie was not completely happy, but remained content the for the five years she resided in Los Angeles.

The country had gone to war. Hitler was an evil force that had to be stopped. It wasn't America's fight, but we stand for human rights and freedoms for all. So, like previous overseas battles, America sent armed forces to help their allies with the argument.

The movie industry supported the effort by producing newsreels that were shown before and after movies. It kept families, friends, and the country informed. The newsreels also promoted recruiting efforts.

Minnie was also making plans to return to Tennessee soon. Sadie had called, and said Miss Betty was preparing to sell the café. Minnie started remembering her time at the Roadside Café in Bean Station, and thought she might like to live the same way Miss Betty had, serving her community.

As the years had passed, Frank's had become known as the place for writers and movie executives to gather. It was said that studio contracts were signed over Frank's exquisite meals. American writers were hired by the local studios to create movie scripts, and often came into the restaurant with their assistants to write, edit, and proofread their stories.

Minnie returned to work as she usually did. The day had been like any other day, except today, she had two tables with men in uniform. They all flirted with her and the other servers. They laughed and joked back and forth. There were a couple of injured among them, and though they laughed too, they were more subdued than the rest.

Several offered marriage proposals to the girls. But being of good humor, the girls would ask, "If I married you, what do I get out of the deal?"

One of the soldiers stood and waved his hand in front of himself. "Why darling, you get all this." Everyone laughed.

The other patrons were good-natured about the commotion the soldiers were causing. Even the celebrities that came in stopped by their tables and snapped photos with them, later to be added to the wall of fame over the bar. They signed autographs, and wished the soldiers safe travels. They smiled and thanked them for their service. It went without saying that most would never return home.

Minnie was in deep thought when she left the restaurant for the day, and was suddenly startled when a gentleman spoke her name.

Standing, he said, "I'm sorry, Minnie. I didn't mean to scare you."

"What did you think you would do sitting back against the wall still as an opossum froze on a limb?!" Minnie huffed, raising an eyebrow at him.

"See, right there? That is why I've waited out here all afternoon," he smiled. "No one from this area of the country talks like that. Now and again I can hear the slur of mountain dialect. Tell me, where're you from? I'm from Clear Creek Springs, Kentucky."

"You don't say?" Minnie's huffed again. "Now, what does all that have to do with me?"

"Well ma'am, if you would allow me, I'd like to take you to a movie, dinner, or some's another place you'd like to go."

Minnie paused, but said, "I don't even know you."

His voice was sincere when he spoke. "Well Minnie, that's where I think you're wrong. When you walked up to our table today to take our order, I knew. I knew that you're the girl for me."

"Now hold on there, what if I have a boyfriend or a husband at home?" she said, her eyebrows raised.

"Do you?" he asked, smiling. Pointing to her hands, he said, "I would bet you don't. There's no ring on that left finger of yours, and a girl like you wouldn't be married without one."

She smiled, as she thought to herself, *He's right handsome.* What was so disconcerting to her was that he seemed to know her, and if she'd admit it, it was like she knew him.

Minnie agreed to meet him outside one of the theaters on Friday evening after work. She would not tell him where she lived right away. Walking home, she kept checking to make sure he wasn't following her.

On Friday, as she showered and dressed for her date, she found herself humming, and smiling uncontrollably.

"Get a hold of yourself, girl! It's not like you have never been on a date before." But it did feel like her first date ever. She was giddy as a school girl.

As she approached him, a big grin spread across his face.

"You're the prettiest girl in this town, Minnie. There's not a movie star that can outshine you."

"Now I know you are joshin'!" she chuckled.

"No, Minnie, I'm serious. I've never laid eyes on a girl as pretty as you. And when you speak, my heart stills because I feel like I'm home."

"Do you flatter all the girls like this? Do they all fall for it?" Minnie smiled a bit.

"Aw now, Minnie, I'm not trying to flatter you. I'm telling you the truth. You're the girl for me."

"Tell me, soldier, what's your full name? Don't you think that's an important item you have left out?" she pointed out. "The girl that has *made you feel like home* deserves to know your name. Don't you think?"

"Elijah Harper. At your service, ma'am."

"Well *Elijah Harper*, don't you think you should buy us some tickets so we can go in to see the movie?"

As he walked toward the ticket booth, Minnie noticed for the first time that he had a terrible limp. His left leg was stiff and straight. War injury, or something else?

He returned and took her hand, placed it on his arm, and lead her into the theater. Before the movie, the newsreel played, as was custom. Elijah excused himself, and only returned as the movie credits began to roll. Sitting down next to her, he handed her a bag of popcorn and a soda.

"Almost forgot to buy these for you."

Elijah had seen enough of war. Just because it was a movie did not make it any easier. And without a word spoken, Minnie got it. She had an intuition about Elijah's feelings and emotions. It was unnerving to her, but she decided to just take things with

Karen E Wimberley

Elijah one day at a time.

CHAPTER 30

Minnie hadn't told Elijah about her plans to return home. She thought if he wanted to stay, that she would want to change her plans completely.

Every moment she wasn't working was spent with Elijah. A lot of their time together was spent having simple picnics in the park. They would spread a blanket on the ground, nibble on whatever she had prepared, and read to one another. Minnie couldn't believe that she had a beau. He was educated, and the world experienced.

Under his outward tough guy act was the softness she most admired. Whenever he became agitated, he would say that the simple sight of her calmed him. Talking about mountain life made them closer. He understood how rough it could be. People were poor, and the younger generations were becoming complacent. Minnie told him how she'd escaped the mountain and why, and Elijah never once judged Minnie. He'd become very emotional as she described how lonely she had been over the years.

She had decided the time had come to tell him that she had full intentions of moving back to the mountain or at least to Bean Station, buy the café, and live out her life there. But before Minnie found the opportunity to bring up the subject, Elijah had sprung his own bit of news.

On one of their park outings, Elijah bent down on one knee, held out a ring, and asked her to marry him. He told her he wanted to be her one and only valid husband.

Tears flowed. Minnie accepted his ring, and they married

in a small ceremony in one of the chapels in the neighborhood church. The girls from work and a few of Elijah's service buddies were in attendance, and it was one of the best days of her life.

Minnie had a few concerns nagging her, but nothing that gave her doubt. She would address them after the excitement died down.

On their first morning as husband and wife, she served him breakfast. She thought, *I'm a wife. I have a husband. Life has been good to me.* And as they sat there staring at one another Minnie started.

"Elijah, I need to tell you something."

"What is it, Minnie? Is everything ok?"

"Yes, I just...just had plans before I met you. Things were great for us, so I put them out of mind for a while. Now I want to talk to you about them."

"Go ahead," he said cautiously.

Minnie took a deep breath. "I was within a few weeks of returning to Tennessee. I was going home to buy the small café that belongs to Miss Betty. I figured she'd made a good living and happily lived alone there, and maybe so could I. Now I have you, and I don't know what to do.

"If they send you back to the war, I want to live where your ship will leave and return. I want to be the one that hugs you goodbye and greets you upon your return home."

Elijah shook her head. "Minnie, they won't send me back. This limp here assures me of that. I can't march or keep up with the troop, so I've received a medical discharge."

Running around the table and jumping into his lap, she started kissing his face all over. When she had finished, he drew her close and did not want to let her go.

"So?" Minnie asked.

"So, what?" Elijah responded.

"So...what do you think about moving to Tennessee and buying the café? I have the money to buy it, and we could have a good life there. It'll be a wonderful place to raise our children."

Elijah thought for a moment, then smiled. "Well, Minnie,

I say we could give it a go. If it makes my wife happy, then I want to do my best to give it to her. I'm sure I can find work to help support us."

"You could just help me run the café," she suggested. "It's something we could do together."

Elijah smiled softly. "Now Minnie, I'm the husband, and it's my place to provide for us, not yours. Your café may very well be a success, but it's my place to find my way and provide for you and our children."

Minnie didn't completely understand his resistance, but she wouldn't press him. He was right. He was the man of their home, and she knew, all too well, that she had no right to force him to work for her.

Packing was a little harder this time. Minnie had accumulated more than she thought. There were still presents to buy for Miss Betty, Lilly Mae, Big Joe, Sadie, and Anna Leigh. Her excitement about returning home and being around those she considered family was her source of energy. The one present she was having trouble with was finding just the right thing for Sadie. What could she buy that said how much she cared about her friend, but also represented California?

She settled on a collection of items. They consisted of a silver charm shaped like the state, a tablecloth with a picture of the state marked with symbols that represented different areas, and an autograph book she'd taken to Frank's and filled with celebrity signatures that she had become acquainted with over the years—she explained they were for her dearest friend, Sadie.

Most had expressed sadness to see her leaving. They took pictures with her that she would one day share with her children and grandchildren as she told them of her time in California. One group picture was taken that she was promised to receive via mail. It would be given an exceptional location in her home in Bean Station.

Their things would be shipped home by rail. Elijah had tried to talk her into flying home on an army cargo plane. They could take advantage of this at no cost, since it was available to him for his military service. But Minnie had told him if God meant for her to fly, He would've given her wings.

Instead, he suggested to her that they drive across the county. He could buy a truck to haul their things, and they could stop along the way and see the sights. This idea she liked, so they promptly found a truck, and returned to the train station to retrieve the boxes and luggage she had dropped off for shipment to Bean Station.

Collecting her bank draft for her deposits would be her final task. She was thrilled to learn she had almost tripled her savings.

They would start their cross-country journey early the following morning, leaving Los Angeles on Highway 66. Their first stop would be in Arizona.

The drive took them most of the day. They had been advised to take a lot of water with them, especially for the Arizona-New Mexico leg. Elijah had also prepared for limited fuel. His time in the service had taught him to always prepare for the worst.

In Arizona, they passed through a ghost town. Most of the buildings looked like they were from the old west. On the west end of the city, there was an abandoned cotton gin and feed store. There were very few homes along the main street. Most of the families in this community were scattered out. Couples had moved here to farm, taking advantage of the wide-open spaces.

Minnie and Elijah chose a spot to spread a blanket and enjoy a picnic lunch. There were no trees about, but the building made a cool shade to help break the heat. After eating, they explored the buildings. Elijah snapped pictures of Minnie with his new camera, a Kodak Vigilant Junior.

Flagstaff would be their next stop. They arrived late into the night, so Elijah chose to find an Inn for their overnight stay. If he'd been traveling alone, his truck would have served him just fine, but his wife deserved better.

They rose early, ate a small breakfast, and continued their journey. They stopped periodically to explore small towns, or just stretch their legs as they drove through New Mexico.

Elijah recorded each place, taking snapshots with his camera. He was creating a timeline of their new life together. The drive was long and exhausting, but they were having the time of their life.

Elijah and Minnie Leigh had decided to stay an extra day in Texas. This would allow them to rejuvenate for the second half of their journey. Elijah had purchased the second map to chart out the remainder of their trip to Bean Station Tennessee.

On Friday, Minnie's excitement began to grow as she realized she was within twenty-four hours of being back with her friends. She was beside herself, and a little nervous about introducing her new husband to everyone. Would they like him? Would he be accepted as she was?

She knew she had grown in many ways as a person, but yet she was still Minnie Leigh, the simple mountain girl. All these past years taught her appreciation for the simple things. She recognized her blessings to have seen and experienced different areas of the United States.

They pulled up in front of the Roadside Café in Bean Station around nine AM on Sunday. She hadn't let any of them know she was headed home. When they entered the café, Sadie said, without looking up, "Take a seat anywhere."

"I will, thank you. It's my home after all."

Sadie turned with such speed Minnie was fearful she would lose her footing. "Miss Betty come quick! Look who found their way home!" She ran over and grabbed Minnie as if she would never let her go. It was the best hug Minnie had ever experienced. A family hug is like no other. It fills you up from the inside with an indescribable joy.

Minnie Leigh's back was facing Betty as she came into the dining room from the kitchen, so at first, she didn't realize what all the excitement was about. As Minnie turned to face her, she nearly fainted from the sheer shock. Once again, Minnie was the recipient of that family hug. This time, she reciprocated more easily. She thought Miss Betty would break her back before she finally let go. Miss Betty gently touched her face, as if to determine if it was indeed her.

"You're here. I didn't think I'd ever see you again," Betty's eyes began to water.

Elijah had stood back and watched the reunion. His heart swelled for Minnie. These people were her family. Blood didn't need to define it for her.

He stepped forward only when Minnie turned to introduce him.

"Miss Betty, Sadie, I'd like you to meet my husband, Elijah Harper."

"*Husband?!* You mean you got married and didn't call, write, or anything?!" Sadie's eyes widened.

"Well, we've only been married few weeks. We married and decided to move home almost at the same time," Minnie explained with a smile.

Sadie and Miss Betty ascended on Elijah at the same time, giving him big family hugs as well. All he could do was embrace them and smile.

Next came the bombardment of questions. "Where're you from?" "What kind of work do you do?" "How did you meet our Minnie?"

Turning quickly, Betty stated, "Wait a minute. Did you say move home? You're home for good? Not just a visit?"

"That's right," Minnie beamed. "I thought I'd move home, buy the café, and raise my children with the only real family I've ever known."

Again, she hugged Minnie. "I'm glad you moved home, but you can't buy the café."

Minnie's heart sank. "Why? Sadie said it was for sale. Did you change your mind?"

"No," Betty shook her head. "I've already sold the café."

"To who? Who would buy a café way out here?"

"I would," Sadie spoke up.

"You bought the café?" Minnie blinked in surprise. "But why? You have a husband, and your letters said he provided well for you and your children."

Sadie's expression turned sad. "Yea, that was before he was killed in the war."

A hush filled the room.

Minnie looked at Elijah with a pained face. "What've I done? I talked you into moving all the way here, and not *once* did it cross my mind what I'd do if she had already sold the café. *Now* what do I do?"

"You can always work for me, Minnie," Sadie suggested. "Business isn't what it used to be, but surely it'll pick up?" she shrugged.

This slightly uplifted the mood in the room. Still, Minnie was ready to introduce Elijah to the rest of the Café family. Taking his hand, she led him into the kitchen to meet Lilly Mae.

"She's not there," Sadie shook her head, her expression sad again.

"What do you mean she's not there? Where is she?"

"Minnie, Big Joe passed about two months ago," Miss Betty told her softly. "He and Lilly Mae been together so long, her heart couldn't take it. Doc said she died of a broken heart."

Minnie buried her head into Elijah's chest and sobbed.

Tired from her long trip, the emotions from her homecoming, and now the hurt over the passing of not one friend, but two, was about more than she could take. Her knees went weak.

Elijah caught her, picked her up, and carried her to a table. Betty went for a cold cloth, and Sadie fixed both of them some hot tea and a bowl of soup. Though her heart was heavy, Minnie accepted the nourishment, and was still so relieved to be home where people knew just how to love her.

CHAPTER 31

Betty quickly spruced up Minnie's old room, and fresh linens were placed on the bed. Elijah and Minnie settled in for the night.

The room was peaceful, and was just what Minnie needed after their long trip, unexpected news of her friends, *family*, passing, and the loss of her plans for buying the café.

Waking early the next morning, Minnie felt refreshed. She dressed warmly, and headed out to the field behind the cabins to greet the day as she'd done every day so long ago. As she walked through the trees, memories of the last time she'd been here flooded her mind. She could smell the smoke from the bonfire, and almost hear the music and chatter of all her friends during her hoe down.

"Good morning," she said, looking up at the sky. The stars and moon remained barely visible as the sky lightened from the rising sun.

"Good morning God. Here I am again, back home. It seems like yesterday since I was last here. I don't know what I'm going to do now that I *am* here. I was sure buying the café was what I should do. Now I'm here with a new husband and everything I own, and nothing to do for work. My little savings won't carry us very long. Elijah tells me not to worry, that he'll find work and we'll find a home. Right now, everything seems hopeless. I'm thankful those that I love surround me. I'll have to trust you to show me what to do."

As the sun began to peak over the mountain, Minnie had the feeling her journey was not complete. She didn't know where she'd go from here. This was the only place she'd ever felt was home.

Walking back to the café, she entered through the back door, as she had done so many times before. She could smell the coffee, and knew that Betty was already up and going. When she rounded the end of the counter, however, she found Sadie standing there counting the tickets from the day before instead of Betty.

"Well, I didn't think you'd be here this early. How early do you come to work?" Minnie asked.

"The kids and I live out in one of the bigger cabins, so it's a very short walk to work."

"You live here too?" she raised her eyebrows.

"Yes," Sadie nodded. "It made it easier for the kids and me. I didn't just buy the café. I bought all the land and cabins too. Miss Betty needed to be free of everything. It all became too much for her to take care of."

Minnie nodded. "I'm glad you were here. I thought I'd be the one to take over."

Sadie frowned softly. "I'm so sorry, Minnie. If I would've known…"

"No need to apologize. I didn't call or write, and maybe it's not where we need to be. Maybe there's another plan for us."

The two girls poured themselves a cup of coffee, and sat down at a table. Minnie told Sadie about living in Dallas, her move to California, and all the beautiful places she and Elijah had visited on their trip home. Sadie told Minnie about her husband, and what a wonderful father and husband he'd been. Sadie's girls knew about Minnie Leigh, but they still hadn't met her. Whenever someone spoke about Minnie Leigh, she was spoken of as family.

After a while, Elijah came into the café, as did Miss Betty. The morning crowd was slow but steady, and as before, breakfast was homemade biscuits, sausage gravy, eggs, bacon, and fried sausage. Homemade jams and jellies were always available to spread over the biscuits.

As Elijah and Minnie sat eating their breakfast, Minnie told Elijah that she'd like to take him to her home in the mountain. She hadn't returned since the day she was traded. She didn't know if her Paw was still alive or not.

Betty walked over and sat down beside Minnie. She couldn't believe that her girl was home. "Minnie, I have a letter for you. It came about a month ago. It was hand delivered by one of your brothers."

Minnie's eyes were wide and confused. "My *brother?!* How on earth did he know where to deliver it?"

"He didn't really. He showed up here and said that word had reached someone that you might be living in Bean Station. He came in and asked if I knew you. I told him I did, but I'd heard you moved off to Dallas. He gave me this letter, and told me if I could help get it to you, he would appreciate it. He had joined the service and was being shipped overseas," Betty explained. "He didn't say much of anything else. I promised I would try and find you and get you the letter; however, I was not sure you'd want to hear from any of them."

Shaking and a little fearful, Minnie took the letter from Betty. She held it in her hand for a bit, trying to gain the courage to open it.

Elijah asked if she wanted him to read it for her. But Minnie shook her head. "No, I'll do it. I just don't know what to expect."

"Would you like to be alone, Minnie?" Betty asked.

"No. Please, I'd like you to sit with me as I find out what it has to say."

Opening the letter, she found the handwriting was crude, and so was the grammar.

Dear Minnie Leigh,

It has been years since any of yourins people have seen or heard from youins. When paw passed on, he told me what he had done. I wish I would have to know'd child. I would have fetched youins myself. Youins and I are the only families left. Three of our brothers were kilt running from the Federals while running Shine. Two of'em were kilt overseas. I never really found out what happened to the youngest. He came up missin and no one's heard from him no more.

If'in you are 'round youins need to know that paw left youins the cabin and all his land. There were pert near a thousand acres 'til the government came in and stole nears three hundred of that away. They say it is to keep it so's visitors can see these mountains as they always been. They're called our mountain, The Smokies. Isn't that something?

Well, child, I hope youins is well and happy. I can't say I will see you again. I might not make it back. If'in you'ins need help with the land go, see old Ernest. He seems to know how to make money from his land, and he keeps the government men from steal'in anymore. There also is a notice at the accessors office, somethin about property left youins by your husband Tolbert Regan, near about 1200 acres. Looks like you rich as the queen a Sheba gal. Like I say old Ernest will help youins if you need it.

I'll be see'in you ins.
Jerimiah Robertson, your brother.

Minnie read and re-read the letter several times. Tears began to fall. She didn't know why she didn't remember her oldest brother very well. An out of focus face, an image of someone talking to her, laughing, hugging.

For the first time, she realized she always thought she would return to the mountains one day, and her brothers would be there, and they would all grow old together with their children and grandkids. Now, she had no blood family. It was a finality she'd never thought about.

When she looked up from reading the letter, Betty was watching her with tears in her eyes. "Is it bad news, child?"

"No, not really." Minnie said. "I just always thought I would one day see my brothers again, maybe even grown old with them. They're all gone now. Jerimiah says, he and I are the only ones left. He also says I own everything that was Paw's, along with what Tolbert left. He's that man Paw traded me to. Must be gone too, 'cause my brother said the accessor has a notice about him leaving twelve-hundred acres."

Everyone was staring at Minnie with their mouth agape, not believing what they were hearing, or how casual she was speaking of her great fortune.

"Well child, let's go see right now," Betty stated. "He needed to give you the whole damn mountain after all he did to you."

Minnie sighed. "Miss Betty, I'm not angry anymore. It was what it was, can't go back to it. Thinking 'bout it won't do anything but make me take back a lot of pain I let go of long time ago."

"Okay, gal," she nodded. "But all I'm saying though, is let's go check on it."

After finishing breakfast, Minnie Leigh, Elijah, and Miss Betty gassed up Miss Betty's car, and headed for Minnie Leigh's mountain. After an hour of driving, they turned onto the mountain highway.

"Lord, child," Betty said. "No wander you were next to complete exhaustion when you reached the café that day. You walk halfway around the world to get away from here."

"I don't recall it being this far. All I was thinkin' about then was gettin' away from the men up here," Minnie shrugged.

Re-winding back and forth on the road as it climbed higher, Minnie frightened them when she blurted out, "*No way!*" She couldn't believe her eyes. "When I left here, there were only two buildings, a mercantile store with a feed store out back, and the postal service was inside the store."

They were now entering a small town, rows of stores on both sides of the road, and parking out front. Anyone that was on the street turned to stare at the strange car as they slowly drove through.

After about a fourth of a mile, the buildings began to thin. "There's a town hall," Elijah said, pointing. "You suppose the accessor is in there?"

"Where else would you find a land accessor in a town this size?"

Climbing out of the car, Minnie led the way into the Town Hall. Stepping to the first desk, she was greeted by a young lady about her age.

"My name is, or *was*, Minnie Leigh Robertson Regan. I received word you'ins had a notice for me."

The young lady smiled. "You're in luck, miss. Your case was going to be closed next week. You would've lost all your land."

Stepping to a file cabinet located in the next room, the young lady pulled a manila envelope out. She removed one sheet of paper from the package, picked up a pen, and laid it in front of Minnie Leigh.

"If you'll sign here. This letter states what day you picked up these deeds. We placed a letter in there along with them. The government will be levying taxes on the property. Cost is different depending on where your land is located."

Minnie Leigh signed after reading the paper. The clerk handed her the package, and they walked back to the car.

"Well Minnie, would you like to see what it is you inherited?" Elijah asked.

"Not sure I want to go back there," Minnie admitted.

"It *is* up to you. But land sittin' is a waste. We can make a good life off twelve-hundred acres, Minnie." Looking at the map, Elijah estimated it would not take long to drive to the homestead area of the property. He noticed there were two homesteads, and chose the closest one.

As they drove, Minnie couldn't place where they were. Maybe she'd never seen this part of Tolbert's property. The road was rough and steep in areas. Driving out of a sharp curve and over and slight rise, they came to an area that was clear on both sides. Looking out of the window to the right, Minnie saw an old garden area. It even had old bean poles sticking from the ground. Her stomach seemed to flop over.

"Stop," she said. Then, *"STOP!"* she almost screamed, opening the car door. Before the vehicle completely stopped, she exited, walked to the middle of the garden area, and looked across the property where it was all as she'd left it.

To the left and twenty yards or so away were the chicken coop, barn, and the corral she'd built all those years ago. Scanning around, she saw the cabin that had brought her so much misery.

Tears welled up in her eyes.

"Do you want to see the cabin?" Elijah asked. But before Minnie answered, Betty shook her head. Elijah didn't understand, but stayed quiet as Minnie slowly made her way back to the car. Turning the car around, they headed out.

"There's another homestead not far from here. If we take this fork on the right, the road seems to go straight through and back around to town. Do you want to drive through this way?"

"Sure," was all Minnie said.

Driving slowly, they could see how high they were in the mountain. Occasionally the trees would thin, and the views were beautiful. Betty could see how Minnie Leigh could miss living in her mountain.

As they approached the second homestead, Minnie couldn't believe what she saw to the right was a waterfall, and to the left was the cabin Ishmael had built.

"Just keep going, I don't want to see that cabin either."

Elijah nodded, then asked, "While we're here, Minnie, do you want to go by and see your old home place?"

"Might as well, done seen my other two," she sighed. "Might as well see the place of my birth."

Now, it was clear to Elijah why she was so upset. The first two cabins belonged to her *husbands*. He didn't know how they'd call themselves husbands; nevertheless, up here, she must've been known as a loose gal leaving not one, but two husbands. Just ran off to God knew where.

As they entered town, Elijah stopped at the accessor's office again. Going in, he asked for directions to the Jerimiah Robertson homestead. The young clerk gave him directions full of landmarks.

After a couple of wrong turns that led to dead ends, and turning around a couple of times, they finally made it.

Pulling up to this sight was not as bewildering as Minnie thought it would be. Walking up to the steps and climbing up onto the porch, she was flooded only by memories of her Paw smiling at her, patting her on her head saying "Come on, little one. Let's tend the livestock," or "Come on, little one. Let's take a hike over to the falls." Minnie was surprised that all she could remember were the good times she'd shared with family here.

"Elijah," she suddenly said, "we're home. Well, if that's ok with you."

Elijah couldn't say no to Minnie. She looked calm, and with the peace he saw reflected in her eyes, why would he want to deny her?

Looking around like he was putting his approval on the place, Elijah just smiled and nodded his head.

CHAPTER 32

"Grams? Grams, are you ok?"

Minnie looked up at her granddaughter slowly.

She felt a little confused at. At first, the memories had been so clear, so present. Everyone was still there. That was the thing about birthdays and anniversary celebrations, they lasted all weekend.

Minnie walked around greeting everyone, slowly making her way to the house. As she hugged Elijah, and reassured him she was okay, she heard car doors shutting. Turning around, she recognized one of the women. The oldest slowly walked toward Minnie, smiling.

"Well, don't stand there with your eyes bugged out! I haven't changed that much. Hair's gone white, and a few wrinkles, but surely that's all."

"Sadie?! Oh my goodness, it is you!" Minnie smiled wide.

"Well, who else would drive up to the top of the world to see you?"

"Only you'ins and my kinfolk."

"Everyone else knows you're worth it."

Minnie and Sadie fell into conversation like they always had. They locked arms and went into the house, away from everyone else. In their hearts, they were still the same two young girls that had met many years ago.

Elijah had become accustomed to this scenario over the years: the greeting, the locking of arms, giggles, and then disappearing for the first few moments of their visits. Today, he was sure their alone time would last a while longer as they reminisced about the years that had passed. Climbing the steps, he took a seat on the porch swing, smiling to himself as he reflected on how blessed he was.

From the moment Elijah and Minnie moved to Tennessee, and things didn't go the way Minnie Leigh planned, he would step up. And step up he did, even though the only things Elijah knew were wood working, and mechanics. Woodworking, he learned from his father, and mechanics while in the navy.

Elijah had carried on his family tradition making guitars, fiddles, and dulcimers. They were each carved from carefully chosen wood found in the east Tennessee mountains. He built a workshop beside the barn, easing the ability to manage both his business and Minnie's farm, though she rarely needed his help in management.

It was the physical demands that she would occasionally allow him to assist with. But his craftsmanship spoke for itself, and as word spread, orders grew beyond a one-man operation. Two young men and a local girl were hired on to help him keep up with the orders. Elijah would prepare the wood for carving, and oversaw the assembly of each instrument. Once dried, he alone tuned and played each one, as it took a gifted ear to know when the instrument had found its voice. He then, and only then, placed a personal letter of guarantee in each box.

Elijah had also designed and built several additions to the cabin that Minnie grew up in. Their four children never wanted for anything. But even though she could give them everything, Minnie insisted they earn their own money to help buy their first car. She taught them the importance of saving, and having a *just in case* fund. They had all earned college degrees from the University of Tennessee, or East Tennessee University. As far as Minnie and her children were concerned, college and earning the degree was more about the experiences and learning how to function in society.

Her oldest son helped her manage her inheritance, and the second oldest ran a small pharmacy and diner in their small mountain village. The two girls were happily married, and chose to teach in the local school, which allowed them the same schedules as their children.

From the original homestead, seven hundred acres were left. It was well known that Minnie had done exceptionally well on selling the timber. This land wouldn't be sold, but it would pass on to the next generation. The property would be protected and guarded by those that followed.

The timber was also cut on the twelve-hundred acres. Minnie Leigh oversaw both cuttings to ensure that the land was not stripped.

As the National Park was formed, Minnie Leigh lost three-hundred acres of the original thousand acres her Paw owned, and four-hundred acres out of twelve-hundred left to her by Tolbert.

In the Late 1950s, Minnie was approached by a land developer. He said with tourism on the rise and population growth, he would, for a fee, manage her land for her. He would make her a millionaire.

Minnie, however, held on to that land for a few more years, and in the end, sold it for more money than her family could ever spend.

It's not well known outside of the mountain community that she'd become one of the wealthiest ladies in east Tennessee history.

She continued greeting the morning and talking to God. It was a journey and still is, learning that He is real.

Elijah had even built her a one-room cabin in the clearing where she could look over the valley. She greeted the sun every morning, and dug Ginseng and herbs. From time to time, they'd go up together and enjoy the stillness. Even though the valley was now scattered with homes, and had a road that ran along the river which ended in a large parking area near the foot of the waterfall, Minnie still thought it to be the most beautiful place on earth.

Minnie Leigh and Elijah stood on the steps of the cabin watching the last of their guests pull away as the sun set across their mountain. Minnie wrapped her arms around her husband's neck, and gently touched his cheek with hers. She loved him more than she ever had.

"Well Mr. Harper, you can't always see the blessings of your life as it's coming together. Sometimes, it can only be seen when it's finished."

THE AUTHOR

K.E. Wimberley makes her home in Alabama and Tennessee. She is a Travel Nurse, and enjoys traveling the US researching American history.

Made in the
USA
Lexington, KY